CULPRIT OF DIVISION

THE NAKED TRUTH

DR. HENRY I. BALOGUN

iUniverse®

CULPRIT OF DIVISION
THE NAKED TRUTH

iUniverse books may be ordered through booksellers or by contacting:

iUniverse
1663 Liberty Drive
Bloomington, IN 47403
www.iuniverse.com
1-800-Authors (1-800-288-4677)

All references to the scriptures cited in this book are from the King James Version of the Bible, except where indicated otherwise. Also, all drawings in this book are provided by Renhay H. and inserted with permission.

Images are illustrated by Renhay H

ISBN: 978-1-5320-9115-5 (sc)
ISBN: 978-1-5320-9116-2 (e)

Library of Congress Control Number: 2020902967

Print information available on the last page.

iUniverse rev. date: 02/18/2020

I am not the person you presented to the world, and you are not the person you portrayed yourself to be. I have no choice but to reject ungodly color-coding, demeaning labels, and many other misleading as well as division-prone things discovered and revealed in this book. The time to set the record straight is now.

It does not matter how long it takes to reject a misnomer as long as you do not lose the courage to say, "Enough is enough."

CONTENTS

PREFACE

A human right is a God-given right. It is a nonnegotiable right. Past attempts by those who felt led or ordained to color-code and reclassify humanity by playing God were relentless. Equally so were those who chose to believe blindly by elevating one group while systematically destroying a large part of the human family. What took place with the blessings of kings and queens as well as religious leaders who were supposed to represent God—along with many others, including the media, who were supposed to point out the truth but did not—was nothing short of an unprecedented act of humankind's inhumanity.

Nothing in this book suggests or advocates expectation of political correctness. This is more than that. Correcting misnomers on a scale never before seen in history requires more than window-dressing. We are all going to need a complete transformation from within. Truth cannot be ignored anymore.

There is no end to learning. It is a continuous process requiring an open mind as opposed to a rigid and cemented one. We may have to tear down and completely demolish an old house of lies in favor of what is true, undeniably real, beautiful, and encouraging.

How do some people live or sleep at night knowing that they are intentionally destroying innocent souls in order to nurture a false sense of superiority and a holier-than-thou attitude? Above all, how do they come to accept what is selfishly uplifting but morally wrong and ungodly? Is it really that difficult to accept the truth? You are about to be challenged to see if you can actually and truly handle the truth.

If it was possible to convince other like-minded people to go along with the twisted stories of the past, do the priviledged group, the self ordained "white supremacists" think they can equally fool God? Perhaps there are some truths you know but intentionally ignored, or maybe they are completely unknown to you. Whatever the case may be, I am going to ask you to keep an open mind, as we are both going to unveil the mysteries of ages. It is a fact that no lie can live forever.

MISINFORMATION AND MISNOMERS

To begin to unmask the truth about a place originally described as "the New World" and now known as the United States is not without some challenges. To think that something this spectacular could be built on erroneous information is unimaginable. To further think that the same erroneous information could ricochet across nations and cultures and divide people against one another is mind-boggling. First of all, I am going to make a daring attempt to start to peel off some misinformation associated with the history of this great land. The United States is significant in light of its unique composition and its dominant influence and strength. It is indeed a country like no other! If a wrong decision is made by the government of the United States, it will vibrate across the ocean and wake up nations around the world faster than the speed of light. A hiccup in the United States' government affairs could have nuclear effects across the globe. As the United States goes, so goes the world. Its significant place in the world makes it extremely important to go after the misinformation I discovered which some people might like to shy away from. Some of the misinformation that might seem irrelevant in our effort to solve the problem of division has plagued a great part of the human family all over the world for centuries As important as the United States' place is in the world, little do most people know that there are some major anomalies in its foundation as well as its history.

In a pluralistic, multiethnic, multicultural, uniquely complicated, and delicately designed to be accommodating and inviting society like the United States, with no prevailing culture or tradition and ethnicity, fact cannot remain contaminated. Getting people to understand its structure in light of the original intent of the founding fathers is complicated but not impossible. Its composition is not without many unintended misnomers and misinformation. Most of the existing misinformation is, at a minimum, self-serving misinformation designed to deceive and derail unity. The United States was not supposed to be a country of one ethnic group and one culture but the land of "we the people." This book is written to sort through, expose, and explain some major misinformation. Disarming the shameful past with the intent to help establish peaceful coexistence is a must-have ingredient for peace and a solution to division.

Misinformation is defined as *false or inaccurate information*, while a misnomer is defined as *wrong or inaccurate label, term, or designation*. Information provided without comparison or thoroughly checked for accuracy could be considered subjective. Information provided as a result of perception could be considered a personal opinion. However, information definitively provided as the truth and recorded as such without qualifying it with a phrase such as *in my opinion* could be classified as misinformation. To call something other than what it is or to label a group of people differently from who they are is a misnomer. Both are wrong, and they do not have to be deliberate or accidental to be wrong. They are wrong the moment they come out and are allowed to linger without retraction and correction.

At times, what we know and what is factual are diametrically opposed, and we wonder how that could be. When the people we hold in such high esteem start spreading falsehoods through the creation of fake news and hammer it with statements such as *believe me*, or *I know this for a fact*, or *people are saying*, and you hear that over and again, you are bound to think that there is some element of truth to it. When the same erroneous information goes on for years, it is bound to look and feel like the truth, and history is full of such information.

It is not uncommon to see a group of people trying to take credit for the effort of many whose unprecedented human strength, ingenuity, sweat, and blood built something as spectacular as the land simply known as the Americas. It does not matter whether involvement was voluntarily contributed or forced through wicked, selfish, inhumane acts of hard labor, servitude, or slavery. What matters is the fact that many were involved and worked tirelessly without compensation. They got involved in building something they hoped to one day call *ours*, with no intent of going back to their original homelands. They all accepted the New World as their permanent homeland. This book explores and exposes who they are, how they got here, what happened to them, and how the evil of hate, prejudice, and division designed to destroy them can be defeated.

To unlock the tangled web of misinformation and misnomers existing and perceived, we need to first understand what is true about the human race as well as all erroneous identification created by those of crooked mind currently existing and falsely accepted as fact. Was there a quick desire to separate one group from the other or a deliberate desire of a people and kingdom to place themselves above the rest? Whatever the reason, was it designed to undermine and sabotage the natural order of things? How does this relate to what is going on in the United States?

First of all, the unexpected stories of natural displacement of many who got caught in the divine plan of land separation, which led to identification of nations, cannot be ignored. The stories of many brave men and women who were in the middle of it all and got pushed into oblivion by science and history need to be unveiled. It is even worse when science makes it look like it happened in a different time. Existence of humankind and what science was able to establish could not agree with theological fact in conjunction with what is true and provable. That opens the door to historical misnomers and misinformation.

Different men and women from different parts of the world got involved in the pursuit of exploration and expansion in the interest of economic development and growth. Somehow, their ambition met with another explorer's desire to be first and rule the world. It thereby gave birth to another level of misinformation established to justify selfishness. The type of misinformation cultivated was, no doubt, self-serving, dismissive, very disrespectful, and extremely disregardful. Nearly everything about other explorers got erased through misinformation but was miraculously preserved to be discovered.

The last phase of misinformation and misnomers covered in this book is in regard to forced labor through slavery. What started in ancient times and was repeated for generations after was repackaged to look like it happened only to one specific ethnic group. To try to shame a particular group of people and force them to own what did not begin with them is not going to make the misnomer and misinformation go away. To say that this type of misinformation is dangerous is an understatement. It is outright deadly and ungodly. It represents the greatest enemy of hope and faith in the future. It was strong enough to stop dreams and eliminate pride in one's ability to do things or pride in who you are. It can easily make people less important and incompetent and can even erase their existence.

On an individual level, misinformation built on fake news is to the mind of humans what atomic energy is to the world—a destroyer on a large scale. Like fake news and innuendos, misinformation is as dangerous as an undetected silent killer, such as carbon dioxide, which can result in death by asphyxiation. Misinformation can push people to commit suicide. If leveled at a group of people, it can lead to unfounded fear of that group of people, or unintentional hate and discrimination by those who are different or outside of that group.

People who embark on misinformation or the spreading of fake news know exactly what they are doing—destroying dreams and aspirations, destroying things, and destroying people. However, to them, the end justifies the means. If they hold on to a specific lie, made-up story, or point of view, it is always to the exclusive neglect of facts, and it does not matter who they are or who is affected. They are not unaware that their extreme lies and innuendos are highly biased, hurtful, and toxic. They are not unaware of the fact that it could go against their faith, divine dictate, or the very basic tenet of their religion. It just doesn't matter. They are not always easy to convince. Most of the time, they are unyielding and unapologetic. They always look for a way to rationalize and justify their actions.

When the truth is finally revealed, they make every attempt to prevent it at every level. The more they talk about their lies and innuendos, the more successful they are at their never-ending distortion of the fact. Conspiracy theories and fake news are everywhere—on the internet, radio, and television, even on religious TV stations. One cannot help but wonder, *When will the inaccuracies, distortion, and outright destruction of facts end?*

Misinformation, even in the land of the free and the home of the brave, can go undetected and uncorrected for centuries. Fact-checkers can be overwhelmed to the point of allowing misnomers to exist as the new norm or simply the new truth. My desire here is to open up a few of them and bring out the truth designed to help establish peaceful coexistence among the human family. It is likely to agitate the sleep of many, stir up resistance and new resentment, bruise the unsubstantiated false sense of pride of some, and simply make some people say, "Is this guy for real?" In the words of Dr. King, "Truth crushed to earth will rise again." the goal of this book is to help breathe life into some of the truth that has been diluted, relabeled, repackaged, and designed to deceive the general public and shame and destroy people using an inferiority complex and unearned suffering.

To emphasize, misinformation is as old as the existence of humankind. Dissemination of fake news, hoaxes, rumors, and conspiracy theories in favor of distorting and tilting the facts, with the desire to shift opinion for selfish reasons, thereby creating baseless biased opinion, makes it important to dig a little deeper. We have seen instances whereby names and logos of mainstream media were used to create the appearance of legitimate and believable news outlets, when in actual fact it was nothing but a carefully orchestrated, false news platform. They are not unaware of people willing to believe anything but the facts. The Swedish newspaper the *Local* called "this type of proliferation of fake news a form of psychological warfare." To allow misinformation and misnomers to continue to thrive in the effort to destroy facts will do nothing but continue to create unmitigated pain, division, separation, and hate.

This book is written to sift through some of the misinformation we have inadvertently entertained for years without the effort to correct it, thereby setting the records straight. Many people, even in the media and academic communities, are not immune. They are as equally guilty as most of those who subscribed to the entertainment of all these misnomers, misinformation, and pseudointellectual displays.

The important role of the United States on the world stage as a real melting pot and the only country truly representative of the world is the reason I decided to embark on a journey intended to dive into some of the misinformation and misnomers. No doubt, the United States provides the yardstick by which we measure integration, truthfulness, and fairness all around the world.

The false claim of the privileged few intended to divide in support of a better-than-them attitude, deeply rooted in baseless assumptions of supremacy and superiority, necessitates the exposure of facts. It is not my goal to elaborate or expatiate on the shameful, dehumanizing, and deplorable stories of the past but to reveal and highlight them in the interest of a better solution than the existing and cancerous division, hate, and discrimination we all rightly, fearfully, or inadvertently inherited.

We are, first of all, going to look at the facts about the human race. Most of what you think you know about the human race and population reorganization, redistribution, and explosion is challenged, completely turned upside down, or discredited in this book. To understand how we got to where we are today, we are going to touch on the three facets of human movement and interactions with one another. The truths about our fellow human beings are exposed like never before. The source of our division is not left out. Get ready to discover the truth about the following:

- continental drift
- exploration and economic development
- the root of division
- the role of slavery

Brace yourself as we uncover what is real and factual about the following:

- continental and national pride
- the United States
- brutality, discrimination, and injustice

Solutions to the division between us lie in the following:

- exposure of streams of division
- peaceful coexistence

Culprit of Division: The Naked Truth is designed to inform people, agitate those who thought they were well informed, and wake up many who have given up on knowing the truth.

THE HUMAN RACE

There is nothing in scientific findings or in theological or historical discoveries to prove that God created different types of people and divided them into separate races, such as *white* or *black*, as currently exist. There was no significant distinction of any kind that we can scientifically, theologically, or otherwise point to or put in place that can justify the assumption of the racist few that one ethnic group is better than the other or superior to the rest. If anything, the Bible says that "God created man in His own image" that is all that was revealed to us, and that is all we know. It is not the goal of this chapter to try to explain how we have come to have different features and characteristics, including pigmentations.

The book of authority as to the origin of humankind is the Bible. The Bible is known as the book of books—the heavenly message to all the human family. It did not portray outward descriptions and depictions of people for a reason. How God sees His creation was not hidden but exposed. "The Lord does not look at the things people look at. People look at the outward appearance, but the Lord looks at the heart" (1 Samuel 16:7). For so many generations, there was simply no reference to the outward aspects of people, such as color of skin. All throughout the scriptures, nothing but genealogy, lineage, and national origin were revealed about people and discussed at length. This kind of color neutrality was divinely employed for a reason. It continued until after 1650.

There was no shortage of those looking to gain recognition through some disturbing, self-serving, unscientific, and clearly divisive studies meant to establish dangerous divisions among the people once referred to simply as *the people of God* or the *human family.* In his 1684 publication *Nouvelle division de la terre par les différentes espèces ou races qui l'habitent* (*A New Division of the Earth*), as revealed by Wikipedia, François Bernier, a French physician, "is considered the first to published post-Classical classification of humans into distinct races." His study was the first to call white *pure* and every other ethnic group *impure.* This and the ensuing ungodly desire to walk in uncharted territory led to the rat race of superiority. To label one ethnic group as *pure* in a study that called another ethnic group *impure* is insensitive and nothing short of an outright rejection of what God created and certified as *good.* There was no logical explanation to support the conclusion of his study other than the fact that it was mainly based on deceitful observation. No doubt, the favored group (the so called "white") is bound to feel happy with the display of some ego and jubilation out of this world. It was not surprising that Dr. Bernier's study, along with its destructive conclusion, went on unchecked for years. It was also not surprising that it served as the foundation for the false pride and weak disposition of the privileged group. The fact that the study and its biased conclusion refused to acknowledge the beginning of humankind and consider a theological explanation and any other available logical possibilities of his day makes the entire study something to reject.

The words *pure* and *impure* with reference to the outward appearance of humans did not appear anywhere in the Bible, and that speaks volumes. Interactions and genealogy are highlighted and often repeated. The fact that skin color was never mentioned tells me it was not important to God. What is even more striking is the fact that nothing is written about it in the Bible or revealed to the disciples; this speaks volumes. To try to understand that through interpretation provided by humans would no doubt set us on an impossible journey of trying to understand the mind of God from the perspective of an individual whose idea of God is unknown.

The word *race* in reference to skin color, creed, or language was never mentioned in the Bible. The Bible could not have been unusually silent or totally ignore the importance of such a delineation and one of the world's sources of selfish pride with no basis in fact. In addition to that, God did not separate people based on the color of their skin and call them to live in different parts of the world because they were from different races. All we know is that God created humans in His own image. The story of creation did not provide us any justification or any support or revelation to support the idea of a white race and a black race, as some people erroneously have been led to believe. The story of creation revealed that God created humans in His own image and provided reproductive mechanisms by which to multiply and populate the earth.

The scriptures do not have the word *race* but the words *human race* and *mankind*. However, one might argue that the word *race*, according to the New International Version, appears in the book of Romans 9:3. According to *Strong's Concordance*, the word *race* in the NIV comes from the Greek word *suggenes*, which means *kinsman*, and *kinsman* is defined as a person *who is one of a person's blood relations*. It does not mean people of different race. When talking about people, the Bible usually refers to the *human race* or *mankind* and says nothing to indicate or refer to physical features or characteristics that can be translated as different races.

Those who think they are superior need to know that they are part of the human race, and the claim of superiority is a false claim. To classify people as a white race, black race, or whatever race, to the point of identifying nations as races, such as the Mexican race, Russian race, or French race, is nothing short of deceptive division designed to diminish the wonderful work of God. It is something designed to produce a better-than-you or holier-than-thou mentality deeply rooted in baseless pride. Race is not defined by skin color; geographical location; human features, such as hair texture, nose shape, and eye color; or other characteristics and national boundaries. Race defines a group with identical traits, bloodlines, behaviors, ambitions, and social desires. Humans, regardless of traits and characteristics, national origin, language, and culture, are considered a group. Unless you can prove that one ethnic group is less human than the rest, the delineation that currently exists is meaningless. Before you disagree with the fact, check your DNA and the DNA of the people you are linked with or related to and see how interconnected and interrelated we all are.

Whether one admits it or not, there are many ethnic groups within the human race, and within each ethnic group are tribes, as in the tribe of Juda, or people who are grouped by language or by land. To say that people are grouped together as a different race because of the color of their skin is a misnomer.

Innate language, culture, and tradition constitute interesting and arresting ethnic identity available to be explored and appreciated. To think that any of these make you of a distinct race is, at a minimum, a serious misidentification and misclassification of yourself. The human race is simply all the living human inhabitants of the earth as a group—the one created by God and in God's image. If the existing variations among all the living human inhabitants of the earth make it difficult for you to accept those who are different from you, and you do not want to see them as belonging to the same race as you, feel free to take it up with God.

With that said, to be a racist is to be antihuman. If you believe that your ethnic group is superior to the rest or divinely ordained to bully the rest of the world into believing your false claim, you are no doubt antihuman and qualify to be labeled a bigot. A bigot, in this sense, is a person who is extremely prejudiced, with an arrogant, biased mind toward another ethnic group within the human family.

Unsubstantiated and ignorant arguments of the past about race cannot be allowed to continue with their baseless, misleading assertions and ugliness. The distinct traits along with the desire for material things in life, coupled with the extreme ambition that exists in one culture but is less significant in another, make us unique and not less important than any other group. No doubt, early jumps on innovation and countless inventions using natural resources along with extraordinary human strength, employed either voluntarily or involuntarily, helped shape our world. Oppressive attitudes and tactics led to the idea of *us versus them* and *superior group versus inferior group,* which eventually led to *our race versus their race.* Nothing could be further from the truth. Distinct identities, such as physical attributes and even geographical locations, do not make any group less or more human than the rest. We are all members of the same and only human race. Any effort to distort the fact is nothing short of ignorant.

Existing variations and characteristics, countless individualized genetic dispositions, and our unique identities are testaments to God's awesome work, and not meant for the divisive *us versus them* mentality. Distinguishing blue blood and red blood is nothing but a further attempt to deceive and establish a false identity. Blood types may be different, but the color of blood remains basically the same.

No doubt, immediate access to financial resources that ultimately translate into immediate access to all other things, including opportunities and access to better things in life, which are wholly responsible for credible research and innovation by most people, fueled the effort of the privileged group since the beginning of the world to the exclusive neglect of others.

A Darwinian attempt at explaining race is nothing short of discrediting God, and I cannot give credence to such a laughable and discriminatory explanation designed to divide instead of unite us. It is like saying that cloning, which is a human attempt at playing God, might one day become another race. Nothing could be further from the truth!

Cloning, which only exists among single-celled organisms, has a better place in reality than the so-called Darwinian evolution. Whatever the argument and its conclusion, the cloning that exists in nature provide a "different processes that can be used to produce genetically identical copies of a biological entity. The copied material, which has the same genetic makeup as the original, is referred to as a clone." Natural cloning exists among bacteria. They are capable of producing "genetically identical offspring through a process called asexual reproduction which is basically a 'lack of sexual attraction, or low or absent interest in sexual activity.' In asexual reproduction, a new individual is generated from a copy of a single cell taken from the existing organism." However, the system of reproduction in humans, as ordained by God, is not through asexuality but through mating made possible by strong sexual attraction.

No matter what effort is made through scientific research at cloning a human, it cannot lead to a new race. Without extractions from existing and living human beings, cloning a human being would be impossible, because it cannot be done without extracting from what God has made. That, by itself, is enough to make any outcome of human cloning part of the human family.

PLATE TECTONICS AND THE CONTINENTAL DRIFT

Figure 1. Pangaea, provided by Renhay H.

From what was once known as *all land* or *Pangaea* emerged what is today known and recognized as continents—the land separated by seas and distance. How did we get here? No doubt, we are living in a world divided into separate and unique geographical locations, such as Africa, Asia, Europe, Antarctica, Australia, North America, and South America, by what we can only attribute as an act of God. We have continents and nations within each continent. In addition, we have areas that are labeled in spite of the fact that they are already part of existing continents. They are labeled in conformity with their chosen identity.

One of these areas is the Middle East, and within the Middle East is the Arab world. Another area is Caucasus (more about this later on).

The phenomena known as plate tectonics (responsible for the split of Pangaea) and the continental drift (responsible for the drift and the distance between them) cannot be ignored. These all-important events provide a window through which to see the past while trying to understand the source of our current population distribution and the origins of people naturally displaced and categorized into various ethnic groups and nations accordingly. The land popularly known as the New World did not come into existence out of a vacuum. Revealing what is logical, factual, and explainable helps us find out what is true about land, people, plants, animals, and culture. It might further help us to know who we are, where we are from, and the original source of indigenes identified in many nations, as well as the aborigines, along with the source of their culture, music, and rituals. It might also help us to see what is true about those labeled as belonging to an ethnic group they had no connection with, such as *American Indians*, who drifted originally from West Africa to the land currently called the United States. It would, at a minimum, help explain the whereabouts of people in an effort to understand the interconnected aspects of the human family, as well as the real composition of America as two distinct continents, along with the United States as a nation within one of the continents.

It is a little difficult to imagine that the world was once compressed into a single protocontinent that Alfred Wagner called Pangaea, meaning *all lands*. Over time, the protocontinent broke apart through a divinely inspired system now known as plate tectonics, and they drifted apart into their current distribution through the continental drift. That, by itself, sounds so overly simplistic of something so complicated but logically and, especially, scripturally true. We can only assume it happened many years ago but not millions of years ago. The timeline is debatable, but it happened. The fact that plate tectonics and the continental drift made a separation of the world into continents possible as we know it today is too amazing to ignore. "Most of the continents seem to fit together like a puzzle. The West African coastline seems to snuggle nicely into the east coast of South America and the Caribbean Sea. A similar fit appears across the Pacific. The fit is even more striking when the submerged continental shelves are compared rather than the coastlines." If you look at the east coastline of the United States, you can see that it was once part of the area that stretched from the tip of West Africa to the northern part of Africa. How the original inhabitants came to be known as *Indians* as opposed to simply *Africans* defies logic. Also interesting is the fact that the nations now known as India and Pakistan broke off and drifted away from between Mozambique, Zimbabwe, and South Africa. The interrelated aspect of humanity is undeniably real.

As recorded by the University of Oregon's website (http://abyss.uoregon.edu/~js/glossary/plate_tectonics.html), "Alfred Wegener explicitly presented the concept of continental drift for the first time at the outset of the 20th century. Though plate tectonics are by no means synonymous with continental drift, it encompasses this idea and derives much of its impact from it."

In Encyclopedia Britannica, Antonio Snider-Pellegrini (a French geographer and scientist) created two maps demonstrating how the American and African continents might have once fit together, and he found identical plant fossils in Europe and the United States. Abraham Ortelius, in his work Thesaurus Geographicus, suggested that the Americas were "torn away from Europe and Africa … by earthquakes and floods" and went on to say, "The vestiges of the rupture reveal themselves."

Figure 2. Before continental drift

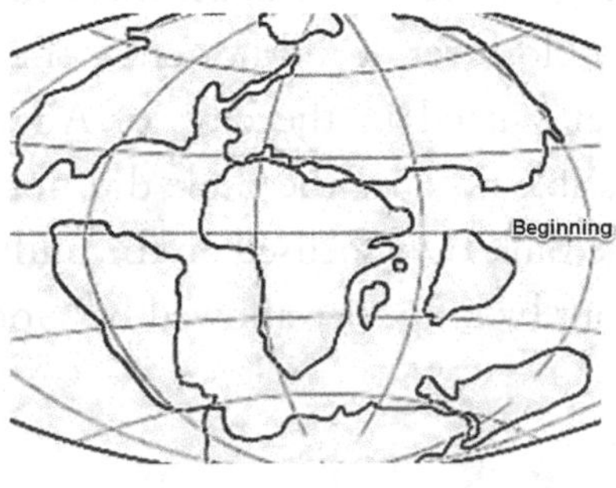

Figure 3. Beginning of continental drift

To say that the continental drift only affected land and not its inhabitants and their culture, vegetation, and various plants and animals is an understatement designed to deny the very existence of people and undermine a theological explanation of creation. The continental drift definitely did not happen before God decided to make man in his own image and assuredly not prior to the actual creation itself but after.

Like other phenomena such as linguistic experiences in Babylon—a phenomenon that clearly marked the beginning of different languages, peoples, and their culture—the continental drift simply could not have happened two to three hundred million years ago. The fact that it happened and as a result of earthquakes and floods tells me that it happened in the time of Noah and around the same time the changes in languages occurred—Genesis 9, 10, and 11. It is the only flood recorded in the scriptures, and it has been discovered and acknowledged by archeology in spite of the fact that science and theology are not always on the same page.

The flood in the days of Noah was like no other flood before it or after it. It was not the type of flood that floods a street or a house. It was not the kind of flood strong enough to uproot houses from their foundation only to dismantle them or push them down the stream. It was a flood powerful enough to break and move mountains and crack and rearrange land, thereby separating lands into nations. It was like putting a final spin on what God had already created. What an indescribable flood brought about by an indescribable, all-powerful, and almighty God. Its impact traveled beyond what the eyes of anyone can see. However, it did not erase the existence of humans or discontinue what started in the days of Adam. It made a population explosion possible because the Bible did not mention loss of life for a long time. The Bible only focused on the multiplication of the human race brought about by longevity allowed by God.

SEPARATION INTO NATIONS, PEOPLE, AND LANGUAGES

I am going to ask you not to speed-read this section as well as the verse in the book of Genesis referenced here. Get ready to be awestricken. This is a great eye-opening revelation about how we ended up with distinct nations, people, and languages but managed to remain as one race—the human race.

The story of the beginning of the world was explicit. We can all attest to the fact that separate nations as made by God and not separate creation different from the offspring of Adam and Eve as resident of each nation is also equally explicit. An estimated year of occurrence of the continental drift cannot make it older than the existence of humankind, which would inadvertently give credence to any unintelligent assumptions about different races, as opposed to one race—the human race. Assigning an arbitrary number of years to an event without consideration to other prior events or phenomena is highly toxic to academic ambition and unacceptable. The only clearly documented evidence of the continental drift ever recorded is in the scriptures. In the book of Genesis 10:5 (NET), the Bible says, "From these the coastlands of the nations were separated into their lands, every one according to its language, according to their families, by their nations." Is that not clear and explicit enough?

The continental drift did not happen in isolation and was applicable not only to land separation and redistribution but also to the migration of people: "everyone according to its language." This also include natural resources as well as the cultural migration of its inhabitants. The original culture of people may have gone through unintended modifications and reorganization because of this natural displacement and migration, but slight similarities cannot be ruled out. The continental drift was not devoid of the strength and determination of people and the willingness to rise above calamities and destruction of a high magnitude.

We not only faced the natural divide as a result of the continental drift, but the world as it existed prior to that changed tremendously. Some would argue that it changed to reflect our new and various locations. Some have truthfully argued that exposure to various climates is partly responsible for pigmentation and certain characteristics that further redefined some of us.

The fact that no one ever tried to argue in favor of a new race makes it significant and something to explore. However, my goal here is to establish the fact that we all drifted from our original place and now exist in our current and different geographical locations. There were some misidentifications of people, but the place of origin cannot be misidentified.

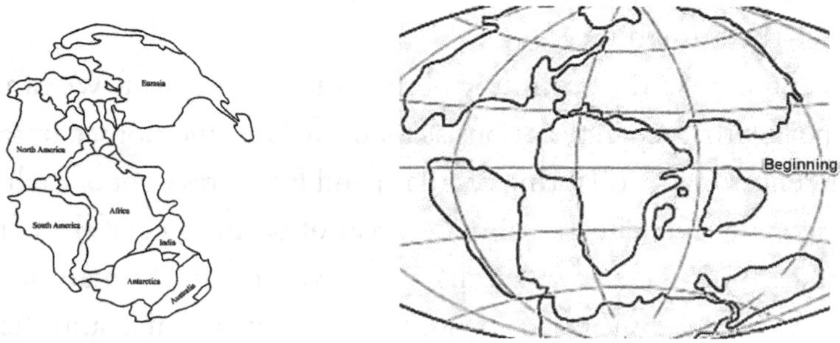

Figure 4. A look at original land and the drift

Before the drift, we were all one people, divided only along ethnic, cultural, and tribal lines. There was no mistaking the fact that many of the existing continents drifted away from the only remaining place at the exact location of the original Pangaea, now known as Africa. Those with a false sense of superiority may not like to agree with that fact and reality, but the indisputable fact remains.

How the world looked before plate tectonics or the continental drift is not a mystery. When you look at the two maps provided above, solutions to the puzzle (as explained earlier) seem to be in plain sight. There are some who would like to twist the truth for selfish reasons in the interest of some weird and ungodly explanations designed to place one ethic group above the rest or simply to confuse and misinform. Many have long accepted their new location and their undeniable connection with the rest of the world, in light of the fact that they are not alone in this world. We are all members of the same human family.

The continental drift by itself did not stop people's desire to want to see what is going on around them, hence the continuation to the second phase of exploration.

EXPLORATION/ECONOMIC DEVELOPMENT

We have to be mindful of the never-ending list of hardships all the early explorers encountered. Part of the expectations placed on many of them was to go and come back home or to make a permanent place for themselves and live happily ever after. It is highly unlikely that they were expecting the "litany of difficulties and life-threatening situations such as unknown hazards, diseases, or even sudden death," hostile reception, greed, and extreme selfishness that can result in sudden termination of life by others. Going to unknown areas can lead to encounters with predatory wild animals or an unfriendly, inhumane, and threatening climate. However, the joy and satisfaction associated with victory far outweighed the hardship and danger. These were not timid men and women but brave souls.

The age of exploration was not unique to whites only. It was an ambition embarked upon by diverse ethnic groups and by men and women. The desire to explore other places or land in the interest of economic growth and territorial expansion was indeed human. This was a desire extremely appealing to people, regardless of ethnic leaning. It was not an idea based on skin color either. It was basically the right thing for the human family to do.

Greed and the expectation of becoming the dominant group may have led to the rat race of selfish ambition, wanting to be first in claiming the *discovery* of an important landmark or river that was first discovered by earlier unidentified explorers. Many of the earlier explorers were not sent by kings and queens; they did not have the ambition, and neither were they out to discover, conquer, and colonize.

The hope of a dynasty was not on their shoulders, and there were no high expectations placed on them and their journey. There was no need to file exaggerated reports or make false claims. Their mission was basically to explore what was on the other side of the ocean, establish relationships, economic or otherwise, and expand. There was no plan to disrupt or dismantle cultures and languages.

Giving credit to only one group of people, neglecting all others, and failing to acknowledge earlier explorers and their tremendous contributions to development and growth, along with failure to acknowledge their whereabouts, was unfair—to put mildly. The neglect is an intentional disregard of their bravery and their journeys, which were not widely documented or were intentionally ignored. The burning desire of some privileged few to be first led to the creation of unchecked false information that made its way into history books, thereby becoming the foundation for greater misinformation. The story of the efforts and bravery that helped reshape, repopulate, develop, and beautify our world could have been told differently and truthfully.

To come up with a chronological order with regard to people and their exploration is not an easy task, especially when you are dealing with history that was distorted and selfishly written. The fact lies in knowing how those before us chose to interact for whatever reasons. One of many things discovered is the fact that before Christopher Columbus, there were the Vikings (as revealed by Christopher Klein on history.com), whose original language was the old Norse. They were probably from Scandinavia or Estonia. Before the Vikings, there were the Africans from West as well as East Africa, as revealed by Leo Weiner of Harvard University. The human family had always been itching to get to know one another, and exploration made that possible.

Exploration was a voluntary venture of many individuals or groups, or a specific family's extraordinary desire to see what was on the other side of the ocean. Kings and queens of some different kingdoms got involved, and everything became marked by extreme ambition and greed. Exploration was a human thing to do when curiosity and the need for expansion started to make us think out loud. It was one of the most obvious reasons to travel outside of one's comfort zone. In the age of limited activities, when entertainment was not on the scale as what we have today with radio, television and internet, socialization was not as expanded. There was more attention to economic growth and exploration. Traveling for fun or to see a relative or loved one was not common in those days.

Exploration ran the gamut of human ambition, desire, and dedication. The tiresome detail of self-imposed accolade along with the desire of some privileged groups to intentionally crown latecomers as the first explorer, because the real first was not *one of them,* is nothing short of a misnomer. How can we put fake news to rest when history is packed with misnomers?

Previous records show that there were tremendous exploration activities five hundred years before Christopher Columbus. One questionable reference about the record is the fact that it was done to the exclusive neglect of the exploration effort made by non-Europeans. In that case, the world knows nothing about other ethnic groups' efforts and contributions to development through exploration. Acknowledgment or praise for a job well done is a good thing. However, as noted by Martin Luther King Jr., "The only time people do not like praise is when too much of it is going toward someone else."

There is buried evidence about the fact that the presence of Africans in the Americas did not start with slavery. Although Africans did not come with the intent to conquer or colonize any geographical area, or at a minimum to transform a culture and take over land, they came as sojourners. Their desire to stay longer than previously planned, or call the new place home, was encouraged by their hosts. As a result, many of them decided on relocation.

Christopher Columbus himself, as revealed by Leo Weiner of Harvard University, noted in his journal how Native Americans confirmed the presence of "black skinned people from the South-East in boats, trading in gold-tipped spears." A Malian historian and playwright, Gaoussou Diawara, wrote about the presence of Africans in America "nearly two centuries before Christopher Columbus's famous landing." In his book *The Saga of Abubakari II,* Diawara "describes an African monarch who abdicated his throne in 1311 and set off to discover whether the Atlantic

Ocean, like the vast River Niger, had another bank." This African monarch "landed in Recife, on the coast of Brazil."

In addition to this, "the thesis of an early African presence in the Americas was prominently advanced by Guyana-born anthropologist Ivan Van Sertima in his 1977 book, *They Came Before Columbus.* Van Sertima argues that Africans reached the Americas in two stages. The first wave, ancient Egyptians and Nubians, reached the Gulf of Mexico around 1200 BCE and 800 BCE, respectively, bringing with them writing and pyramid-building. Centuries later, around 1310 CE, the Mande people of West Africa went to Mexico, Panama, Ecuador, Colombia, Peru 'Cuba,' and various Caribbean islands, according to Van Sertima. The Olmec stone heads of Mexico, which have astonishingly African features, are among the archaeological and linguistic evidence Van Sertima presents."

As revealed by the United States history provided on the internet, Spanish explorers came years after and did not hesitate to make known their interest in the west coast of South America. Credit was given to Vasco Núñez de Balboa as the individual who discovered the Pacific Ocean in 1513. Other explorers followed, and the desire to claim any preexisting landmark or geographical area—in the interest of being the first to discover it and creating a lasting impression at home—was just too tempting to ignore. As a result, they put their names on whatever was there prior and disregarded those who came before them. Many of them returned home only to be told to go back and govern a specific and defined area.

French explorers, according to the source, came in packets of smaller groups and landed and settled in many places. They were not as concerned about coastlines as the English were. Their efforts differed tremendously. They were not afraid to go into the deep interior regions. They prided themselves in "developing thriving commercial interests, especially fur trading and fishing, rather than planting large permanent settlements."

According to "French colonization of the Americas" provided by Wikipedia, "Samuel de Champlain, the greatest of the French explorers, founded Port Royal (1605) and Québec (1608). Jean Nicolet (Nicollet), a companion of Champlain, explored Lake Michigan and surrounding areas in the 1630s. Louis Joliet and Jacques Marquette conducted explorations of the Mississippi Basin in 1673." Everything was done to promote French interest, regardless of original intent.

My main interest in highlighting efforts and interests will not permit me to dwell so much on a particular group and their underlying reasons for exploration.

From German explorers in the New World to the presence of Ivan Fyodorov and Mikhail Gvozdev of Russia in Alaska in 1732, people never stopped looking for opportunities, excitement, economic growth, and territorial expansion through exploration. No single effort is more important than the other. They all deserve recognition and their rightful place in history. If the question is whether or not those early explorers were educated enough to be truly called explorers, it depends on how much you know about the beginning of education.

The oldest university in the world, as provided by Guinness World Record, is the University of Karueein, founded in AD 859 in Fez, Morocco, on the continent of Africa. After that was the University of Bologna, Italy, in Europe, founded in 1088. In those days, you couldn't embark on such noble missions of exploration if you were completely illiterate or ignorant.

SLAVERY, HATE, AND DIVISION

The beginning of the New World did not escape the unspeakable horror, brutality and ugliness associated with servitude and enslavement. It inevitably translated into hate, division, prejudice, and discrimination, which eventually catapulted all over the world, and one ethnic group became the beneficiary. The monumental task of carving out a new nation, powerful and truly pluralistic, within an existing continent certainly did not go without the uncomfortable and at times forceful displacement of people from all over the world.

Whether or not you agree, the establishment of the New World could not have happened without some divine intervention. The fact that it was initiated by those identified as settlers, along with their desire—selfish desire—coupled with some wicked, inhumane, and at times barbaric ways of bringing people from all over the world, voluntarily or involuntarily, is too much to ignore.

Slavery brought the third wave of Africans to the Americas. The first wave was the displacement caused by the continental drift, and the second was due to exploration as a result of the desire of many to see the world around them, for experience, and to open trade in the interest of economic growth. The third wave was one of shame, anger, and the degrading of people once full of pride and hope. Slavery, needless to say, was one of the most dehumanizing acts of humans. It was, no doubt, a human dilemma—a highly disturbing and uncomfortable way of asking people "to come over to Macedonia and help us." To pull people from their comfort zones and force them to do things they would not have agreed to do otherwise was just too provoking, to say the least. To twist facts in favor of a better-than-them attitude and then turn around to blame the victim is an ungodly act.

If you are aware of the story of slavery, you should know that it did not start with black people, and it definitely did not end with black people, but black people became the beneficiary of never-ending, unearned suffering and its lingering brutality. It, no doubt, changed destiny. It robbed many people of their dignity and left them with a diminishing return. To receive such dehumanizing treatment and a tarnished image was not the choice of those on the receiving end. No one wanted to give up comfort, freedom, and dignity. Unfortunately, it was taken without much consideration to the feelings of the unfortunate recipients.

It is shocking to know that some of what we have come to know about history is historically false. What is real and true has been selfishly twisted, changed, and covered. The worst part is the fact that individual opinion and willingness to passionately defend one ethnic group against another have allowed the truth to be surgically and methodically removed in favor of a "we were treated better than them" attitude. However, the truth, though crushed to earth, remains undestroyed for inquiring minds to discover.

The first wave was never mentioned anywhere, and the second wave was disregarded in favor of the desire to be first. This shows how resentment of a high magnitude can help bury the effort of many people. The story of slavery reveals that not all white people in America came as free men and women, and not all black people in America came as slaves. The ability of the privileged group to control what was disseminated through different and available channels, most especially printed media in those days, helped suppress history. There were free men and women on both sides of the aisle, and there were slaves as well.

The unspeakable horror and cruelty of slavery in England came out of the fact that King James II and Charles I were at the forefront of the effort to enslave others. They captured and enslaved lots of Irish even before the journey and the discovery of the land that was later named the New World.

In an article published by John Martin in *Global Research*, an online publication of March 2015 titled "The Irish Slave Trade—The Forgotten 'White' Slaves," John revealed that "they came as slaves; vast human cargo transported on tall British ships bound for the Americas. They were shipped by the hundreds of thousands and included men, women, and even the youngest of children."

Without going through all the gory details of the ugliness of slavery, the fact remains that they were brought to the New World as slaves. Some people would like to argue against the fact, because they believe those Irish slaves were simply indentured servants, not slaves. If a person "is bought and sold, chained and abused, whether for a decade or a lifetime," that qualifies as slaves.

History.com reveals that "Irish slave trade, in North America as a continent, started when a lot of Irish prisoners were sold as slaves to English settlers in the West Indies." As a matter of fact, "the Irish were the main slaves sold to Antigua and Montserrat in the 1600s." It grew so quickly that about "70% of the total populations of Montserrat were Irish slaves."

"When looking for more slaves, the British settlers would go to Ireland, the biggest supplier!" In addition to the Irish, other whites were enslaved in large numbers. It was not a secret that "the early slaves to the New World were actually white" people. The atrocity was beyond sinful; it was ungodly. The ugly side of slavery did not respect family or children. It ripped them apart, and the slave masters did not allow husbands to bring their wives and children to the New World.

In his article titled "More on Irish slaves in America," Justin Swanström reported that "During the 1650s, 'a great number of' Irish children between the ages of 10 and 14 were forcibly taken from their parents and sold as slaves in the West Indies, Virginia and New England. Another large number of Irish (mostly women and children) were sold to Barbados and Virginia while some Irish men were sold to the highest bidder. In 1656, Oliver Cromwell ordered that some Irish children be taken to Jamaica and sold as slaves to English settlers." They were not regarded as servants but slaves.

The slave trade involving Irish continued for more than a century. A large number of other white, black, and brown slaves followed. They were considered latecomers and no doubt fitted into a system already developed for enslavement. However, these mixed bags of new slaves quickly gave way to a betrayal of a high proportion.

According to the open computing facility of the University of California, "In 1619, a Dutch ship, the White Lion, captured 20 enslaved Africans in a battle with a Spanish ship. They landed at Jamestown, Virginia for repairs from the battle. For food and supplies, the Dutch traded the enslaved Africans to the Colonials as indentured servants." That quickly changed, and they were dehumanized, shackled, broken, and extraordinarily humiliated to submission. No doubt, others followed, and they came to the New World from various points of no return. The way back to Africa was impossible, and the hope of returning was lost forever. Their condition quickly became deplorable, hopeless, painful, and bleak, as their nightmare seemed endless. The hope of a brighter future was quickly covered by a thick darkness.

There is no official record to support some of the exaggerated claims of so many historians as to the population of slaves or indentured servants from Africa. One put his number at 12.7 million, which would have set it at odds with many official records available to justify the truth. You simply have to wonder what the population was of Africa in 1619. Not only that, how did 12.7 million people get here? How did they make it across the ocean in spite of the fact that transportation on land was nonexistent, and transportation on sea was extremely risky and dangerous? Also, official records obtained from the United States Census Bureau put the total population of the United States when recording started at about four million. "The total population as returned in 1790 was 3,929,214." One would expect the total population of the United States one hundred years earlier (in 1619) to be a lot less than that. See appendix 3. The total estimated population of Africa as a continent in 1600 couldn't have been more than fifteen million. Where did the 12.7 million slaves come from, and how did they get to the United States? The total population of African Americans in the United States in 1790 slaves as well as free men and women, according to the US Census Bureau, was only a few thousands total—a little more than 757,000, and that was exactly 171 years after the first batch of slave ships landed in Virginia in 1619. See appendix 3. What happened to the exaggerated number of 12.7 million people?

In colonial America, as per the same statistics of the University of California, "indentured slaves did not only consist of Africans, but a large majority of them were Irish, Scottish, English, and Germans who were brought over from Europe, and were paying their debt for the passage over sea." Just like other ethnic group, many Africans did not come to the New World as slaves. Many were already on the continent of the Americas as a result of exploration and trade. They came with their wealth and their young men and women, along with many things to help them live comfortable lives. They came as free men and women. Most of them had slaves who were not Africans but white—yes, white slaves owned by Africans. In addition, "Anthony Johnson was one of the first African Americans to have finished his services as an indentured servant and became a landowner on the Eastern Shore and slave owner himself." The number of African slave owners was not just a few but many, and they covered a large part of the New World, including the southern part of the United States as well as its East Coast. There were many African slave owners in Virginia and South Carolina and a few (about seventy-five) in North Carolina.

It proportionately and alarmingly grew to the extent that lawmakers (who were also slave owners) could not accept the new reality, and they decided to do something about it. They came up with a law to control and eventually stop the number of African American slave owners, as well as affect the number of white women who were in love with many African Americans. (See appendix 1.)

The settlers did not turn to violence as a protest of choice. They did not try to appeal to individual African slave owners to free those who are whites and held as captives. Their selfish desire to end African ownership of white slaves led to seeking redress under the law. Legislators met and came up with the law (shown in appendix 1) to help them end slavery but not for black slaves—mainly to end ownership of white slaves by the so-called black people.

To seek redress through legislative action in the interest of bringing an end to something tells me it was not an act of just a few people. It, no doubt, confirms the fact that there were many African slave owners of white slaves. Many of the settlers were slave owners themselves, and while they were hanging on to their slaves—white, black, yellow, and brown slaves—they somehow decided to selfishly stop African slave owners alone, through legislative action.

White slave owners of African slaves grew in number, and the number of Africans in slavery increased beyond what was formerly available, but not as many as some numbers have shown. As more whites were escaping slavery, more Africans became entangled in the new mess. White slaves started to take a shot at becoming slave owners of Africans. When a black slave trying to escape was captured and returned to whoever declared one missing, whichever one was returned was good enough. It was common to say, "They all look the same to me." Names and forms of identification were not important or required.

According to one official record, out of so many African Americans in the United States in 1865 (about one hundred years after the official record started), a great deal remained in slavery. Although some were able to escape, they were not able to enjoy freedom until Reconstruction, even though Reconstruction did not completely fulfill its obligation to African Americans. The fates of almost one million free African Americans, most of whom were slave owners of white slaves, were hanging in the balance. Disappointed would be an understatement. Many did not know what to do. Post-Reconstruction resentment and political party hesitation, including carefully orchestrated, unforeseen objection, did not happen in ways that made anyone suspect something sinister was about to happen.

Reconstruction was supposed to define true freedom and equality of life, but a lot of African Americans looking for unconditional inclusiveness were about to find out how diabolical and crooked the minds of humans can get. The strenuous debate over who was an American, the nature of freedom and equality, and what rights all Americans should possess and enjoy went on. The longer it went on, the further the reality of the debate was for many, especially African Americans. Regardless of the view of the Northern whites versus Southern whites, and regardless of the intended outcome, African Americans insisted on claiming their rights as citizens and insisted on participating in the debate about their future.

Part of the underlying reasons for the prior civil war in the United States had to do with slavery. Abolitionists in the North were all in favor of abolishing slavery. However, agriculture in the South was the main reason many Southerners were in favor of the practice. Expectation of what might happen under Abraham Lincoln was of tremendous concern for the slave owners of the South. As a result, "Seven Southern slave states formed the Confederate States of America before Lincoln was inaugurated." Some Southerners with no economic or any other stake whatsoever in defending slavery decided to side with the Confederacy, and the nightmare was about to deepen for many African Americans.

Sympathy for the abolition of slavery in the Confederacy was nil, and resentment in favor grew a lot larger than expected. Robert E. Lee, a Confederate general, once called slavery *a moral and political evil* but still managed to conclude that Africans in slavery were "immeasurably better off here than in Africa, morally, socially, and physically." No one knew that was not just an innocent personal opinion but a unified voice of many in the Confederacy. The magnitude of those words and how those words and other words would eventually impact life was about to be seen on a larger scale.

In 1863, President Abraham Lincoln issued an executive order titled the Emancipation Proclamation, which was meant "to change the federal legal status of more than three million enslaved people in the designated areas of the South from *slave* to *free*." It brought joy, hope, and greater expectation. The fact that slave owners within the Confederacy would not let go meant that those held in slavery had to escape to experience freedom. Without delay, they started on that route, but the Confederates had another plan, which eventually led to the intent and tremendous plan to destroy. They meant to instill fear and let people know what might happen if anyone dared to step out and help any African American. Their goal was to prove that whites were superior to blacks, and the word *supremacist* was born.

Without wasting time, they formed what is now widely known as the Ku Klux Klan. It was a loaded name to not only prove the supremacy of whites but also avenge for two things—the enslavement of whites by some Africans and the sudden freedom earned through executive order. The words *Ku Klux* derived from the Greek word *kyklos,* meaning *circle*, and the Scottish-Gaelic word *clan*. Their original intent was to make sure that *what goes around comes around*. Making sure things came full circle was not a goal but a watchword. The modus operandi employed by the group was mainly violence and the intent to inflict maximum pain.

They were not interested in civil disobedience requiring public protest. They were not interested in purchasing services they needed to keep their agriculture thriving. They were interested only in asking for the services of Africans (the people they believed were stronger) through violence and force. They were willing to take whatever they wanted by force. The Bible says, "The thief cometh but to still, to kill, and to destroy." "Former Confederate General Nathan Bedford Forrest was the KKK's first grand wizard. In 1869, he unsuccessfully tried to disband the KKK after he grew critical of the Klan's excessive violence," but it was too late.

The Klan's claim of superiority could not come up with a better, civilized, and superior way of dealing with fellow human beings. Instead, they decided to employ evil tactics of inflicting maximum pain, torture, and even death. It showed not only how inferior they were but also how evil, arrogant, and antieverything godly they were. In short, nothing in their modus operandi promotes superiority—only extraordinary inferiority and poor, pathetic, uninformed business strategies. They failed to know that you cannot force people to buy your stuff, provide services, or help you in any way. It takes a superior mind, skills, and knowledge to know what to do.

Everything about them and their operation proved that they were actually the inferior group, hence the desire to cover their faces when trying to carry out their evil plan of lynching, burning, and shooting fellow citizens, people they knew who possibly socialized with members of the same race—the human race. Their outright rejection of God's work, along with their barbaric and inhumane approach, clearly showed that the public acceptance of members of the KKK as part of the human family was nothing short of a mistake.

Their animallike actions served as a stain not only on the good people of the South but all over this great land and the world at large. It drove an unintended wedge between Africans and Europeans. Privileged white business owners had no choice but to subscribe to brutality. They were forced to reject services to black people publicly and privately—in restaurants, in amusement parks, in accommodations, in employment, in public education, in politics, in public bathrooms and at water fountains, and in every facet of human interaction.

They, the white non-Confederate members, did not know how the so-called Confederates might react. The Confederates managed to plant fear, prejudice, discrimination, and hatred in the minds of the people. A lot of people became unwilling participants. The Jim Crow era of many years afterward got so crazy, and "segregation now and segregation forever" became the slogan of many.

J. Edger Hoover, who was the director of the FBI (a federal law enforcement official), refused to obey federal law in enforcement, hiring practices, and equal opportunity. Many school officials did not hesitate to voice their resentment, refusing to admit African Americans for higher education. Many store owners could not resist telling black people, "You are not welcome here." Black people became forsaken, abandoned, and rejected and were pushed into the background in every aspect of life in their own country. Many were thrown into McCarthyism even before McCarthyism!

It is difficult to understand the Confederacy and their sister organization—the Ku Klux Klan—without looking at the other hate group before them. One of those greatly highlighted by history is the Aryan Nations. In an article published by Cristian Violatti in *Ancient History Encyclopedia*, the term *Aryan* is derived from the Sanskrit word *ārya* (noble or distinguished). It represents a "self-designation used by the Vedic Indic people who migrated into the Indian subcontinent about 1500 BCE."

In one of the editorials written and published by the editors of *Encyclopedia Britannica*, the following came out:

> In Europe, the notion of white racial superiority emerged in the 1850s, propagated most assiduously by the Comte de Gobineau, and later by his disciple Houston Stewart Chamberlain, who first used the term "Aryan" to mean the "white race." Members of that so-called race spoke Indo-European languages, were credited with all the progress that benefited humanity, and were purported to be superior to "Semites," "yellows," and "blacks." Believers in Aryanism came to regard the Nordic and Germanic peoples as the purest members of the "race." That notion, which had been repudiated by anthropologists by the second quarter of the 20th century, was embraced by Adolf Hitler and the Nazis.
>
> In the late 20th and early 21st centuries, many white supremacist groups used the word Aryan in their name as an identifier of their racist ideology. Those groups include the Aryan Circle (a large group that had its roots in the Texas prison system), the Aryan Nations (a Christian identity-based hate group prominent in the late 20th century), and the Aryan Brotherhood (a group originating in San Quentin [California] prison). That association with racism, crime, and Nazism has given the word a powerful new negative sense.

One cannot but ask, Why did all former slaves and former slave owners turn against black people? Sons and daughters of Irish descent who were, no doubt, former slaves and sons and daughters of other whites who were former slaves managed to shake off the shame and blemish of the past. A lot of them managed to become a force to reckon with in business, public service, finance, entertainment, technology, education, literary work, the media, agriculture, and scientific endeavors, including real estate, because of extraordinary opportunities extended to them everywhere. Somehow, the effect of the Confederacy and their intent to make blacks pay for what they did not start remains a huge monkey on the back of every black person—men and women—in America and in some cases elsewhere around the world. Why?

Confederate soldiers who believed in maintaining the status quo fought against freedom, citizenship, and voting rights being extended to African Americans, even though they had been here for many years before Christopher Columbus and before the slave trade started. The objection of the Confederacy was carefully planned and orchestrated. Their hateful and public disregard for the executive order signed by the president was meticulously planned. They managed to instill fear in many people all over this land.

In the beginning, the objection of the Confederacy was based in part on the fear of losing African Americans who were slaves. Where would they find anyone with the kind of unbelievable stamina of the Africans? Where would they find anything close to their untiring effort and strength on the field, along with their unwavering sense of accomplishment and the desire to please people even in the face of unforeseen abuse? All these qualities, which originally started earlier, as far back as 1700, became attractive and a magnet for others looking for field workers. By the same token, it was one of many sources of attraction and a reason for the secret desires of some white women later, magnified in the same 1705 law passed in Virginia. "The law contained some modifications on the punishments placed on white women who bore a mulatto child and white individuals who married a person of 'African and other ethnic descent.' The legislators made it clear that Christianity was not the path to freedom for a slave." (See appendix 1.)

The gain of continued enslavement for Southern farmers, in their own assessment, outweighed any other risks. Setting those Africans free by the Declaration of Emancipation was just too much to handle. To pay them for their services would have made many of them rich beyond measure. It would have also made them viable members of their communities and a business force to reckon with.

Instead of positive and humane strategies that could have been highly beneficial on both sides of the aisle, it brought jealousy. Some whites, most especially members of the Confederates, decided to falsely prove that they were superior in every way, and the white supremacist ideology spread like an inferno. A lot of ungodly tactics that I cannot overemphasize enough, such as denial of equal rights and denial of access to education, businesses, finance, careers in entertainment, and accommodation, and extreme discrimination followed. As a result, black people became alienated in the nation they worked so hard to help build. In the words of Martin Luther King Jr., "It is a cruel jest to say to a bootless man that he ought to lift himself by his own boot strap."

Evil got into the affairs of men in ways never imagined. The fear of the Lord disappeared faster than most people could even say the word fast. The spirit of comradery gave way to suspicion. Trust vanished, and lack thereof was visible in every interaction and contact. The question concerning who those people in masks were remained fearfully unanswered. They had to cover their faces to burn friends' houses, drag them out in the middle of the night, and lynch and kill them. Friends turned against friends. Neighbors turned against neighbors. Confidants of yesterday turned into enemies in the twinkling of an eye. The Confederacy gave birth to hate, discrimination, and the evil pride of supremacy on a scale never before seen or experienced in history.

The Confederates' dark, cold, callous, unrepentant, and evil operation went on for years, and the children of light were all on the sideline with passive attitude. Where were those commanded to *let their light shine*? Where were those not afraid to be coworkers with God? Where were those divinely commissioned to love unconditionally—to be followers of truth and ambassadors of Christ? Many are still yet to be seen! The following are the words of James Russell Lowell:

> Though the cause of evil prosper, yet 'tis Truth alone is strong
> Truth forever on the scaffold, wrong forever on the throne
> Yet that scaffold sways the future, and, behind the dim unknown
> God is standing in the shadow, keeping watch above His own.

CONTINENTAL AND NATIONAL PRIDE

To recognize where you are, proudly identify with it, and never misrepresent who you are is a virtue to emulate. The fact that the United States is located on the continent known as North America and not the continent known as Europe cannot be overemphasized. However, the misplacement of truth along with intent to deceive in the interest of a hateful agenda coupled with unprecedented prejudice and arrogant propaganda is making it difficult for a few people in the United States to accept the fact that they are no longer living on the continent left behind by their foreparents but on the continent on which they were born. United States is not in Europe but in North America, and the citizens of the United States cannot claim or identify with Europe any more than they can claim or identify with Africa.

Continental identity and national identity are two different identities that should not be mistaken for any reason. Let us take a careful look at how people relate to their natural habitat on the continent where they are located.

AFRICA

Africans (black or white) are the most notorious when it comes to continental identity. The glow and beaming pride on their faces about the place once called Akebu-Lan, Mother of Mankind, or garden of Eden but now known simply as *motherland* or *the birthplace of humankind* is unmistakable. Haters may see it as a *dark continent* or as the epicenter of everything negative, including poverty and disease, but to an average

African, there is simply no place like home and no place like *the land of blessing.* Unless you really want to know which country an average African is from, the answer is always the same, "I am an African," and they leave it at that until you ask, "Which country?" The color of your skin and the language you speak, including your specific culture and political or religious leaning, are as important as those things may be and are basically not as strong as the binding tie (Africa)—the continent of *warm* and the *rising sun*.

The continent is much more important than the country, and what people think about it or how they see it just does not matter. Africa is so important; they formed the Organization of African Unity. They have, among other things, all African game as well as lots of cultural events. Some Africans were forcefully taken and removed from the motherland. Lots of natural resources were illegally removed and taken around the world, yet the glory remains. Nothing to regret. Many things that could have diminished the glory of the continent through misinformation happened, but its shining light remains forever shining—without blemish. Africans simply refuse to be shamed or discouraged. *Dark continent* is a label deeply rooted and grounded in hate, and all the many negative synonyms dictionaries and people came up with to describe the birthplace of humankind grew out of the desire to overshadow the glory of Africa and the pride of Africans. Those things remain baseless and far from the truth.

ASIA

Second on the list of having continental pride are Asians. They know they are from Asia—a continent of forty-eight countries. Russia and Turkey, although in Europe, recognize the fact that parts of their land connect with Asia.

Asians are proud to identify with their continent regardless of what country or part of Asia they are from. Even in one of the birthplaces of civilization (Egypt), although on the continent of Africa, a tiny part (about 10 percent) of Egyptians believes they are in Asia. How we are all interconnected is undeniably real. Our separation, made possible by the continental drift, makes us not a separate people but distant relatives blessed with unique characteristics and cultures.

EUROPE

Europeans magnify their pride for the whole world to see, and they appreciate their identity as simply Europeans. The European Union is more than just a symbol of pride; bit is a bridge of unity eliminating cultural divide in the interest of one European continent.

Europe, although unique in its ambition and racing desire to colonize, control, and spread its version of civilization all over the world, still manages to respect its individual ethnic ambitions and respective singular craving for power and the desire to be first. Europe's quest for a better way of doing things, a better solution to whatever problem faces humanity, as well as a way to make life better, has led to unprecedented pride. As they are not unaware of the fact that much of what they try to perfect did not originate in Europe, it has made them think that they must be different from the rest of the human race. Their bond, the European Union, was the envy of the world until some began to entertain a false notion of supremacy, which led to the label of *third world* for those outside of Europe. This is a new way of saying *inferior world* without using the word *inferior*. It also led to the idea of *we are different from them and they are different from us*. This became the new modus operandi, which eventually led to false identification of different races.

ANTARCTICA

Antarctica, on the other hand, has no countries, cities, or villages. Ninety-eight percent of the continent is covered by ice. There are various scientific research stations sporadically located and operated by various countries all over the continent. When you look at the image of Pangaea, it is difficult to believe that Antarctica was once part of the land known today as South Africa.

AUSTRALIA

Australia is comprised of fourteen countries and twelve dependent territories. The countries in Australia are Australia, Fiji, Kiribati, Marshall Islands, Micronesia, Nauru, New Zealand, Palau, Papua New Guinea, Tonga, Tuvalu, Samoa, Solomon Islands, and Vanuatu. The dependent territories are American Samoa, Cook Islands, French Polynesia, Guam, New Caledonia, Niue, Norfolk Island, Northern Mariana Islands, Pitcairn Islands, Tokelau, Wake Island, Wallis, and Futuna. On the continent of Australia, continental identity is a confusing subject. Some of the countries and dependent territories are linked, and they identify with other continents and countries. The dominant country remains the torch bearer.

AMERICAS—NORTH AMERICA AND SOUTH AMERICA

America, on the other hand, was never united. No effort was ever made to that end, hence the lack of continental identity. Many of them are unaware they are Americans. What could have been the two most powerful continents on the planet gave way to the bullying ambition of bigots who are unaware or, at a minimum, refuse to believe that they are not in Europe. They like to identify themselves as *the original Europeans,* as if to say that those in Europe are fake. They have no idea which country they should identify with in Europe, and no one knows why they outright refuse to proclaim connection with their continent of birth. The pride of those selfish few for not letting go and continuing to hang on to what was supposed to be a former home is the reason for not recognizing the New World the way it should be recognized. America is not just a continent but two continents.

The citizens of the United States are no more Americans than those in Chile, Bolivia, Brazil, Peru, Argentina, Canada, Mexico, Cuba, and all the remaining countries on the two continents. To say it differently, all the people of North America and South America are all Americans. The United States is one of many countries on the two continents known as America. Exclusive claim to the name *Americans* is a misnomer if it is done to the neglect of other countries on the two continents. However, if it is done in the interest of a better way to describe and identify US citizens—because the word *Yankee* and other ethnic-oriented references are too limited and neglectful and do not give credit to those whose blood and sweat helped define history—it needs to be changed. The vast representation of other ethnic groups in the country cannot be overlooked. On the other hand, if the United States' claim on using the name *Americans* (a name meant to describe citizens of the third and fourth largest continents) was done with the intent to claim the name exclusively, as it currently stands, it is, no doubt, ignorant and selfish.

Migration of people from different parts of the world as a result of the continental drift, along with migration due to exploration is apparently evident in the overall composition of people on both continents called America. To emphasize this truth in the interest of understanding, many people from different ethnic backgrounds are on these continents as a result of the continental drift, or as a result of exploration, or being transplanted voluntarily or involuntarily from different parts of the world. The unique combination of people and their cultures and languages makes the two continents extraordinarily special and different in many ways. "I am an American" belongs to all the citizens of both continents.

There are so many things to be proud of about the two continents. The two continents have a lot in common with the land they drifted from. The rich cultures of the citizens of North and South America are spectacular. The vast natural resources and loving people, who are very accommodating with an inviting spirit, are indeed enviable. Many countries on the two continents are doing fine individually, and many could benefit from inclusiveness. With natural resources such as cotton, soybeans, tobacco, cocoa, banana, and wheat at their disposal, along with a vast variety of mineral resources, such as coal, iron ore, bauxite, copper, natural gas, petroleum, mercury, nickel, potash, and silver, the two continents are undeniably rich. Underutilization may be partly responsible for lack of benefit to the vast majority of its citizens.

The Americas, under the shadow of the United States, have not been able to find a common ground. They have not been able to find a way to unite, recognize differences, and band together as one people. The United States would like to impress on the world that they are the only Americans, and nothing could be further from the truth.

Whatever it is, the United States, totally separated from its own continent, has become a platform to transform the world. It is not uniquely established for one specific ethnic group or skin color but for all God's children. The United States is both a nation and a platform for innovation. If you can start something in the United States—such as nuclear energy, space exploration, advancement in medicine, flight innovation, computer technology, improvement in entertainment, new or better marketing strategies, including hate and division among the children of God—it will spread like an inferno all around the world. In some cases, it might be perfected by a nation willing to embrace the same innovation brought to life on the US platform, built on the freedom to innovate.

EARLIEST GROUNDWORK OF DIVISION

There is an area now regarded as part of Europe, but it would have loved to have been separated. This area, which was originally known as Caucasus, was not big enough to be called a continent but instead a region. However, the inhabitants of Caucasus usually refer to themselves as Caucasians. One of the characteristics that gives them the European identity is not a known or identifiable characteristic but a bold claim in line with European thinking. It is an unfounded claim of superiority. People who believe they are Caucasians believe they are different and better in many ways. By some strange coincidence, the inhabitants of Europe also believe that they are different and better. Somehow, they did not have one word along with the willingness and the desire to describe and embrace the epic shift in skin color. They cannot accept any available explanation with regard to different shades and obvious differences in outward appearances among the human family.

The fact that people are generally referred to and identified by their country or continent of origin remains a fact. However, for a region to offers a new identity to those assumed to belong to that region, in spite of the fact that there are many countries in that region and citizens of each of those countries already have a distinct national identity along with a continental identity as Europeans. This defies logic. The fact that this new identity coexists with the real identity of those from Europe as Europeans shatters common sense and insults intelligence. One cannot help but ask endlessly, "What is the reason behind this unholy alliance?" You will soon discover that later in this book.

Geographically speaking, Caucasus covers an area between the

Black Sea and the Caspian Sea. It includes most of Armenia, Azerbaijan, Georgia, about 10 percent of Russia, and perhaps 15 percent of Turkey. They are mostly concentrated in the area now known as the Caucasus Mountains, located on the border between the continents of Europe and Asia. The so-called Caucasus "is one of the most linguistically and culturally diverse" places on earth. The map presented below shows the area now known as Caucasus.

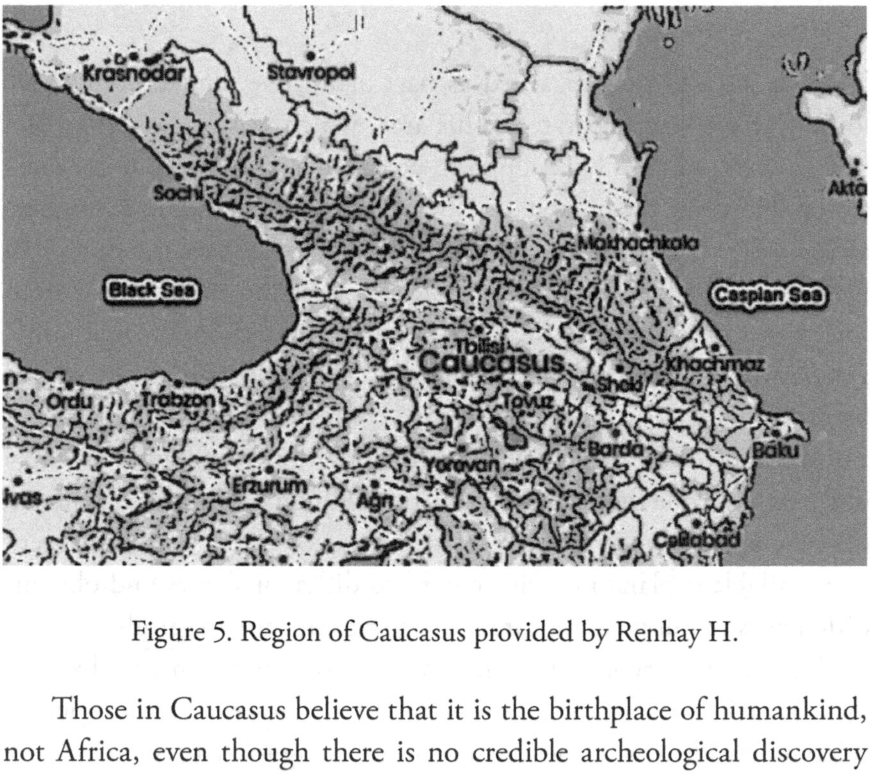

Figure 5. Region of Caucasus provided by Renhay H.

Those in Caucasus believe that it is the birthplace of humankind, not Africa, even though there is no credible archeological discovery to support this assumption. There is also an unsupported assumption that this was the resting area of Noah's Ark, known as Mount Ararat. Regardless of what anyone thinks or believes about the actual location of Mount Ararat, humankind did not begin with Noah; rather, humankind was preserved through Noah's obedience to God. If this was the location of Mount Ararat, please remember that Mount Ararat was not the birthplace of humankind. Rather, it was the garden of Eden, and the actual location of the garden, also known in the Bible as the "garden of God," remains debatable (Ezekiel 28:13).

We have seen some phenomena to support the idea that the garden of Eden was possibly fragmented and distributed or moved to a different location or many locations. If you believe that "the earth is the Lord's," you will also believe that He can do whatever He likes without asking for human permission or endorsement.

Mind-blowing evidence found in Nigeria—yet to be thoroughly examined by scientists—has been found about this real, pristine, magical, and mysterious place, popularly known in the Yoruba land where it is located as "Igbo Olodumare," or in English as the "garden of the Almighty." How they came up with that name defies logic. All I can say is that flesh and blood did not reveal that. The English interpretation, no doubt, agrees with scriptures. This unique place is worth looking into in the interest of discovery. Curiosity and the hunger for what could be true necessitate that we explore every possibility. This is something about the garden of the Almighty that has never been done before, because the entire continent of Africa is considered as simply a "dark continent" as opposed to a better label reflecting what Africa is all about: the birth place of humankind or the motherland.

Going back to Caucasians, they also believe that they

- are the only people created in the exact image of God;
- are superior to any other person on this planet;
- are of a different race, and all other ethnic groups are inferior to them;
- have exclusive rights to the planet Earth; and
- have no known connection to Africa.

It is amazing that Caucasians embrace Christianity but refuse to subscribe to any connection or reference to Abraham, Isaac, and Jacob, hence their disdain of any individual or group of people connected to Abraham, Zionism, or Semitism through lineage. They are unrepentant in their claim that Caucasians are superior, even though the claim is not rooted in fact. There is no known chronological beginning or explainable lineage and no explanation as to whether they believe they originated from Adam and Eve or another creation.

They also claim that they are Christian, but the beginning of their version of Christianity is unknown. For this reason, we cannot establish whether they even believe in Christ, who is commonly referred to as the "Lion of the tribe of Judah." However, the claims of "original birthplace of humankind" along with "original inhabitant of earth" remain just claims with no basis in fact. Their connection to Adam or to the human family is basically unknown.

Their claim was strong enough to lead to the effort that was popularized by a German atheist (an individual with anti-God beliefs, sentiments, and leanings) by the name Johann Friedrich Blumenbach, who in 1795 decided to color-code humanity, thereby completing what fellow atheist Christoph Meiners started earlier. Johann went as far as to divide the human race (the only one race in existence) into five distinct categories:

1. Caucasian, the white race
2. Mongolian, the yellow race
3. Malayan, the brown race
4. Ethiopian, the black race
5. American, the red race

This marked the beginning of a false and hateful racial division, along with an insane characterization of inferiority, which was the culprit of dehumanization, unspeakable torture, pain, and even death of a very large population of the human family. I have to reject his baseless, biased, and people-pleasing division sanctified by many dictionaries on steroids. The fact that the motive behind his erroneous and ungodly label was never challenged by scholars, theologians, or any God-fearing individuals is mind-boggling, to put it mildly. As a Christian and a child of God, I have no choice but to henceforth reject his unscientific assumption. It would be wrong for me to continue, from this point on, to subscribe to this insanity. I cannot overemphasize the fact that this has to come to an end in the interest of a better and divinely ordained solution. The time to end division is now.

As revealed earlier in this chapter, the inhabitants of Europe, including those who identify with Indo-Europeans, generally believe that they are different and better. How did many of them come to believe that they are Caucasians? Was it because of Johann Friedrich Blumenbach, or was it by convenient and ungodly association even when there was no credible connection to the region known as Caucasus?

Needless to say, Europeans already have an undeniable identity irrespective of nation of birth, with no provable bloodline or other connection to Caucasus. Original claims of the Caucasians were magnified by many unsubstantiated conspiracy theories. Their efforts helped justify numerous baseless assumptions, and no one cared to see if any of them were true or fabricated.

When you look at the underlying reason for the pride of those who rushed to embrace the division created by the work of Johann, along with his unjustified label of the word *white* as an identity of choice to group Europeans and Caucasians together, you cannot help but conclude that part of the reason for aligning with Caucasus as opposed to Africa is largely based on intentional effort by that group of atheists to derail the plan of God. It is partly emboldened in this common saying: the enemy of my enemy is my friend.

has no concrete ap[illegible]ed in the [illegible] and divinely ordained solution. The stage to end division is now.

As revealed earlier in this chapter, the inhabitants of Europe, including those who are [illegible] Indo-European [illegible] believe that they are different and [illegible]. How did many of [illegible] come to believe that they are [illegible]? [illegible] when there was no [illegible] Christ.

Needless to say, [illegible] magnified [illegible] to [illegible] [illegible].

W[illegible] the [illegible] Africa is [illegible] the [illegible] end.

NAKED TRUTH

Unless you can successfully prove divine intervention in this unspeakable horror of division (at the hands of atheists) that has plagued and terrorized the human family for years, any further attempt to continue to legitimize this act of inhumanity is ungodly and sinful. Let us ask ourselves, Is anyone really white or black, as explained in many dictionaries? This is not a rhetorical question but a real, legitimate, and soul-searching question. This type of thought-provoking question deserves an in-depth look at the meaning of the word *white* as well as the word *black*, along with the origin of both in reference to the outward appearance of any member of the human family.

To understand this, let us set aside all biases and distortions presented by dictionaries. Let us also set aside all inherent hatred, assumptions, innuendos, outcomes of popularity contests, personal opinions, unsubstantiated family stories, rootless emotional reactions, conspiracy theories, and ungodly comparisons to species that are not human, including all demeaning quasi-scientific research we all grew up with. If ever there was a time to set the record straight, now is the time, and this is the time to sincerely and realistically agitate the sleep of evil.

As revealed by Dr. King, "truth crushed to earth will rise again." This jealousy-induced plan of the devil to set all God's creation against one another turned out to be a well-thought-out, well-orchestrated, carefully executed, gigantic plan. It found receptive allies among those looking for any way, legitimate or not, to boost their ego. It also found a receptive ear among those who are highly interested in making themselves better, greater, and superior to the rest. The undeniable fact remains that we are all colored people. White is a color as much as black is a color, and in reality, no one's skin color includes black or white because nobody is actually black or white as per the dictionary definitions.

Although there are different outward appearances and shades, no one is black, impure, or subhuman, thereby evil and deserving of derogatory words meant to dehumanize members of the human family. This fact needs to be carefully unwrapped, and I would urge you to take a deep breath and go through this chapter with an open mind. Baseless pride and division need to be dismantled.

The race for color delineation gained credence during the quasi-scientific research of the eighteenth and nineteenth centuries. The meaning of *white* as it exists in reality is "pure," with no "spot or blemish," or free from "moral impurity and always in comparison to things that are good, innocence, honesty, and cleanliness." The only individual ever qualified to be identified as "without spot and without blemish" is Christ. No one else can compare. Many of the selfish meanings associated with the word *white*, and its distortion in dictionaries currently in existence, need to be set aside and ignored.

The "spot or blemish" mentioned here is not referring to any skin problem requiring the attention of a dermatologist. This spot or blemish is one of an unspeakable stain on purity. One of the objects here on earth, not man-made, that genuinely qualifies and meets this definition of white, as exists in reality, is snow. Is any human being as white as snow (forget about gray hair, which we often refer to as white hair)? White or gray hair comes with old age, and that is not unique to any specific member of the human family. We all have it. Another question to ask is, Is any human being without spot and without blemish? If you find any one person like that, you are, in fact, looking at a human being without sin—one that we can say is 100 percent pure and equal in every aspect to Christ.

If you believe in what the Bible says, that we are all "born into sin," you may find it difficult to come across anyone without spot and without blemish. If you also believe that the Bible is the Word of God, it will be difficult to make God a liar. Before you get so emotional with the intent to take the law into your own hands, please remember that "it is a fearful thing to fall into the hand of the living God."

White, as it exists in reality, is also symbolic of righteousness. It is the brightest and lightest of all colors and achromatic in the sense that it exists without hue. It is not applicable to any human being and thereby does not meet any of the current selfish dictionary definitions of the word *white*. It is without hue because of its visible and blinding electromagnetic radiation or wavelength. White is often associated with perfection. It is also the most preferred color of most religions and is assumed to be the preferred color of angels.

Concerning the word *black*, the actual meanings are strength, resilience, tenacity, endurance, divinity, and boldness. For some unknown reasons, dictionaries unanimously define it as completely opposite of white, evil and a symbol of poverty. One important fact to emphasize here is that the devil himself was described in the Word of God as a being who epitomizes beauty. He was not given any of the demeaning interpretations attributed to the word *black*. His beauty, along with his gift, as revealed in the scripture, gave him his rebellious confidence and the desire to entertain his ambition to try to elevate himself above God.

Somehow, according to these currently existing dictionaries, black represents everything to scorn and stay away from. To disparagingly define a group of people created in the image of God as impure, evil, and dirty—and their place of origin as a dark continent—is in sharp contrast to the way God Himself sees His creation.

To say that this ungodly label by itself is strong enough to create unsolicited division, continuously fueling this insane fight for superiority and permanent separation among the children of God, is an understatement. Black is believed to be a blemish of high proportion, and there is no other choice but to reject this label that I do not subscribe to. God, the Creator, did not use derogatory labels to describe His creation, which He personally inspected and certified as "very good," according to the book of Genesis. I am simply not black, as defined by some crazy dictionaries, and you are not white. If you have any problem with the work of God and His stamp of approval and certification on me as "good," do not hesitate to it take up with Him.

Let us set aside all distortions and human tampering in reference to the words *white* and *black*. These words are not meant to create division among God's creation in any way, shape, or form because they were not made as labels for anyone. They are not meant in reference to human beings. Neither is meant to demean any group of the human family while exalting the other. Neither is meant to describe the inhabitants of any continent, country, or geographic location. They are just among the color choices available to us and are supposed to be taken at face value for what they are, with no divine approval to use any of the two disparagingly.

The word *Caucasians* originally emerged and was released to the general public in the 1780s by members of the German-ordained Göttingen School of History. It was also mentioned in the "Outline of History of Mankind," written by German philosopher Christoph Meiners, one of the prominent members of Göttingen School of History. He was also an atheist who later became the favorite intellectual ancestor of Hitler and his Nazis. Christoph published his work in 1785 and spelled the word *Caucasian* in German as *Kaukasischen*. This was in reference to the people of Caucasus and was the first to describe them as a different "race," in agreement with one of the false claims of the Caucasians with regard to who they are.

The quest for broader acceptance of the ungodly division among the children of God prompted those itching for a way to justify their claim of a separate race to group all Europeans together and call them white, which means pure, and Caucasians by association. It is somehow amazing and surprising to see Indo-Europe and the Horn of Africa, including North Africa, included. It is equally amazing and surprising to see many of those places dropped from the list when eugenics (which became the modus operandi of the Nazis' unyielding belief) was developed and introduced in the United States by Francis Galton in the late 1800s as a method of supposedly improving and purifying the human race.

ABANDONMENT OF A HIGH PROPORTION

This unhealthy, evil alliance was responsible for the unspeakable division between the so-called black and white or majority and minority. They tried to drag God into their council as a charter member when their plan (developed by atheists) was wholly and without hesitation embraced by the Church of England and nearly all religious groups, including members of those religious groups. The Church of England was not the only religious organization to be active on the side of division. Catholic, Baptist, Episcopal, Methodists, Orthodox, Anglican, and Evangelical churches actively and, in some cases, passively sided with evil and division. They woefully failed a large number of the human family.

Those religious organizations were not the only ones with blood on their hands. All dictionaries decided to demonize, dehumanize, and marginalize Africa, including anyone with linkage to Africa in their DNA. That was not the only thing they did; they intentionally and misleadingly made those classified as Europeans and white as superior. Those classified as Africans and "black" were made inferior by default. They were able to accomplish this because of attracting and tempting definitions accorded to the word *white* by many dictionaries, This, no doubt constitute an ungodly alliance. In essence, every dictionary inadvertently helped legitimize Europe and the Caucasians as superior to every member of the human family, even though there is nothing in reality to support any of the outrageous claims.

Every media outlet knew the truth but decided to take a side, thereby helping to spread misinformation and divisive messages. Financial institutions went with division and denied Africans the privilege of realizing their dreams through borrowing. Educational institutions did not accord equal opportunity to a very large part of the human family. Entertainment industries turned their backs. They even went as far as to portray every biblical figure as European, even when theological and archeological findings were not on the side of such division.

They had forgotten that Africa (Egypt, Ethiopia, and many other places) is also the land of the Bible. A lot of institutions around the world turned their backs on Africa. People in general, even light-skinned

Africans, turned their backs on Africa and fellow Africans. They went as far as refusing to identify themselves as Africans.

For the most part, a great number of the human family willingly and intentionally went for unrelenting demonization and division among a large part of the same human family. Law enforcement officers did not swear to protect and serve Africans but to kill them. The judicial system was largely unfair to Africans, thereby refusing to do justice. Africa was not only looted but demoralized, dehumanized, and marginalized, and they were killed in record numbers.

QUEST FOR A HOMELAND

If you are from Europe, you can be referred to as European (you already have a homeland). If you are from Africa, you can be referred to as African (you already have a homeland). If you are from Asia, you can be referred to as Asian (you already have a homeland). If you are from America, you can be referred to as American (you already have a homeland). By the same token, anyone can be referred to by their country of origin, such as those from France as French, or those from Spain as Spanish, or those from Italy as Italians, or those from Nigeria as Nigerians, or those from Egypt as Egyptians, or those from Mongolia as Mongolians, or those from Ireland as Irish, or those from Japan as Japanese, or those from China as Chinese, and those from England as English. To have no specific homeland, no country or continental identity other than regional affiliation, only to turn around and call themselves Caucasians defies logic. It defies it even more so when there is no known beginning and no biological connection to humanity other than the selfish and isolating claim of "we are the original people" coupled with intent and desire to claim superiority.

UNANSWERED QUESTIONS

One question still remains unanswered by the supremacists and white nationalists in the United States. The question comes out of their irrational demand for a separate homeland for white people. One cannot help but ask, Is that really a legitimate demand? There is this (unintended) connotation of homelessness of the so-called white people that's prompting advocating for a homeland. Did they really understand that everybody in the United States is from somewhere around the world and thus had a homeland prior to coming to the United States? Here is something to remember: different people fleeing tyranny, oppression, and religious persecution ended up here, not with the intent to establish a homeland for white people. In our quest for something new, we formed the land of "we the people" and not the land of the supremacists and white nationalists.

The next question goes to the Europeans, individually. This is a necessary question that must be answered singularly and not as a group. In his book *Moral Man and Immoral Society*, Reinhold Niebuhr emphasizes the importance of individual decisions in the interest of a better solution to problems of society. "It is a historical fact," Reinhold Niebuhr wrote, "that privileged groups seldom give up their privileges voluntarily without some resistance. Individuals may see the moral light and voluntarily give up their unjust posture, but … groups tend to be more immoral than individuals."

Please bear in mind the havoc that division has caused among the children of God, and you will see why this is such an important question. The first part of the question is simply this, "Are you all Caucasians?" Which is to say, "Are you without a homeland?" The second part of the same question is "Are you white, thereby pure and without spot and without blemish?" None of these should be difficult to answer unless you believe that the answer rubs on your pride because you are pure, holy, and equal to Christ in many ways.

Remember this: you are not a bunch of vagabonds; you have a homeland, as pointed out earlier. You are not considered as equal to God. The word *white* was stamped on you without hesitation and legitimized by dictionaries on steroids and by atheists (ungodly researchers) who had no regard for the existence of God. They went with their biased theories without taking into consideration the true and out-of-this-world meaning of the words *white* and *black*.

In the United States and elsewhere around the world, Africans should be proud enough to call themselves Africans, regardless of how they look on the outside and regardless of their religion of choice, without establishing further division. Europeans should be proud enough to say, "I am a European." Same with Americans, Asians, and any other ethnic group. How intelligent you are does not have anything to do with your outward appearance. Rich and poor folks exist in every culture and ethnicity. It is not subject to how you look on the outside. You are not prone to crime because of where you were born or grew up. Oppression, deprivation, evil obsession, and lack of opportunity can sink anyone's dream and aspiration, thereby affecting how some people seek and go after the good things of life.

Division is a terrorist's ideology. They believe in it and hope for it. Division has terrorized and turned humanity against one another for centuries. We can unanimously say to the evil spirit of hate and division, "Enough is enough." We can embrace nonviolent ideology or embrace annihilation in our selfish quest for separation, isolation, and supremacy. Whatever the choice, the United States is not the promised land of the so-called white nationalists and supremacists.

THE TRUTH ABOUT THE UNITED STATES

The United States is unique in many respects—a country like no other. It is the third largest country and the third most populated country in the world. It does not exist along one culture, people, or skin color. Its chosen language could not have been more suitable in light of the fact that the pool of its populace is from different parts of the world. It is the real microcosm of the world. It does not belong to the Europeans, Africans, Asians, or any specific ethnicity or group of people but to "we the people." It is not the property of any group. With that said, it is not wrong to say, "This land is your land; this land is my land." The false claim of "we are the original Europeans" coupled with "we are the only true Americans" remains just that, a false claim. Regardless of where you are from, you are in the land of "we the people," living on the continent known as America. The claim of entitlement belongs to all. Europeans are here, some voluntarily and a great deal involuntarily, but they are here. Africans are here, some voluntarily and a great deal involuntarily, but they are here.

We do not know its original name, but the land was once called the United Colonies and is now known only by its new name—the United States. The land that was once completely occupied by people, before Pangaea, was connected to West Africa, but later (after the continental drift) they were mistakenly identified as simply Indians. No one knows exactly why they allowed the name to stick in light of their original location and connection to Africa before the continental drift, but that's all we know.

Many countries of the world exist with a common identity, such as people, language, culture, and religion. However, the United States came into being as a result of the joint effort of people who were looking for something different and better, who were looking for the type of freedom that never existed anywhere prior and will ever exist anywhere after. The desire to escape tyranny, oppression, religious persecution, and injustice became the driving force behind the idea of "we the people." The freedom to think, to express what is on your mind, and to worship God as divinely ordained in the biblical concept of free volition were extremely appealing.

In spite of its chosen name, the United States was far from united in the beginning. It was more of *us versus them* (divided at every level)—the privileged group versus not so privileged, and the haves versus the have-nots. It was a country divided and on the brink of losing the backbone of its strength and unintended structure and composition. However, its preferred political ideology (democracy) provides a platform for people to come together and express their wants and desires, a platform to choose what is good and acceptable in the interest of building a better place, a platform to speak in unison with one voice through the ballot box, and a platform deeply rooted and grounded in a divinely inspired constitution designed to never change but serve as a foundation on which great ideas and the spirit of tolerance and stronger unity are to be built.

The bedrock of US politics is democracy, and the religion of choice—not imposed—is Christianity. When George Orwell came up with the concept of Judeo-Christian values in 1939, it was mainly meant "to describe Christianity in an ethical (rather than theological or exclusively in liturgical) sense." It immediately became a new way to describe the foundation on which the United States was built, with no intent to misrepresent or mislead anyone.

As for politics, the United States is neither the birthplace of democracy nor the largest democracy in the world but the torch bearer. Democracy, which is the government of the people, for the people, and by the people, was more appealing to those desiring to escape oppression, tyranny, and extreme hate and persecution. They could have chosen a different form of government, but they unanimously decided on democracy. They probably looked into all the available options of their day, such as monarchy, but they did not want to be ruled by kings and queens. They could have gone for aristocracy or oligarchy, but they did not want to be ruled by some rich folks or a group who believe that they are ordained to rule. Dictatorship was another choice, but its totalitarian approach—along with the crushing blow to opponents, freedom of expression, and all opposing views—makes it unattractive and unappealing. Being a democratic republic was another choice. It is neither democratic nor republic but a new way of redefining dictatorship. In light of all the choices available to them, they decided on democracy, with Christianity as the religion of choice—hence "in God we trust."

No matter how you slice it or want to argue the fact, the United States is built on Christ the solid rock. This is one of many reasons the founding fathers declared their unwavering allegiance to God and not to humans or ideology. This fact cannot and should not be entertained on the platform of *maybe* or *how do you know?* It is evident in every facet of the United States' foundation, construction, and development. However, when you look at the fact that the same country gave birth to hate and division on a scale not expected among the people of God, it makes you wonder.

Democracy and Christianity make the United States a pluralistic society. Democracy puts governing in the hands of the people, for the people, and by the people. Christianity encourages and echoes the need to "love your neighbor more than you love yourself," to "do unto others as you would have them do unto you," and to always strive "as much as lies within you, live peacefully with all men." There could be no better combination.

The pluralistic composition of the population of the United States, although complicated, goes deeper than you might want to believe. Freedom of religion is not the same as freedom to govern. The fact that you are allowed to worship God in any way you so desire is protected as your God-given right. With that said, it is important to dig deeper into why Christianity and democracy are inseparable. Christianity is very accommodating and 100 percent operates on the free volition of the people. You can choose to reject it, and nothing will happen to you. You can say whatever you want to say about Christ, and nobody will drag you out of your house to be hanged or beheaded. You can disagree with any evangelist, reverend, bishop, or even the pope, and you will live to see more days, enjoy the goodness of the Lord in the land of the living, and later win the election and become the president of the United States, even after throwing dirt in the face of Christianity. There is simply no need to fight another human being for God. The one who came "that they might have life and have it more abundantly" cannot and will not be the one to advocate the taking of life. The desire to obey God, follow Jesus Christ to the letter, and love your fellow human being more than you love yourself cannot be compromised. You are either a Christian or you are merely professing Christ as Lord, but "your heart is far from Him." Any religion with less concern and love for the human family cannot operate successfully and in favor of all within a democratic society. The two are inescapably and intricately bound together.

The United States is very accommodating and welcoming and still inviting people from all over the world: "Give me your tired, your poor, your huddled masses yearning to breathe free!" But that should not be misconstrued. The United States remains the same, but being a melting pot makes it susceptible and a magnet to diverse groups—good and bad. Evil and greed got in. Wickedness and selfishness snuck in and took over. What was supposed to help humanity became a weapon of destruction against one of the ethnic groups who worked so hard and fought valiantly with their sweat and blood for its existence—all because of who they are, which was divinely ordained by God.

BRUTALITY, PREJUDICE, AND INJUSTICE

Brutality and injustice are widespread problems that should be of concern to every member of the human family. It is the devil's way of depriving us all of the kind of love that was divinely ordained. Brutality is not limited to rough handling or knowingly denying people their constitutional right of innocent until proven guilty. Brutality is unfortunately embedded in our day-to-day interaction. To understand brutality and prejudice, we have to step back to a little more than 150 years ago.

The civil war finally came to an end in June 1865, after the last major Confederate Armies surrendered to the United States in April 1865. Many people were happy at the victorious end in the attempt to defeat inhumanity. The North won. To say that the Confederates were angry at the defeat they experienced was an understatement; they were furious and vowed never to go quietly into the night. As a result, they decided never to let go of their original opposition to end slavery. The executive order known as the Emancipation Proclamation, signed by President Lincoln, was not a deterrent. Civil disobedience was not enough to describe their reaction; it was total defiance. Many people considered the Confederate reaction, which was designed to retaliate against African Americans, as simply a form of expression protected by law. That was the beginning of a problem many of us would like to pin on police officers. Brutality is not limited to law enforcement officers. Remember that part of the oath of the law enforcement people is to protect and serve.

After the war, and most especially after the executive order signed by the president, it practically became unlawful to hold anyone in slavery. However, some freed slaves were still afraid of their slave owners—black or white. The natural instinct of many was to look for a way to not be tricked into going back in spite of the dictate of the law.

Shortly after the Confederates organized the Ku Klux Klan, the devil's hit men, successions of violent reactions toward African Americans and their sympathizers erupted like a volcano and spread like an inferno. The covering of faces along with cross burning by people who were not bold and courageous enough to show their faces (but cowardly covered them) were considered forms of expression protected by law. If it was limited to covering of faces and cross burning, it would have been okay. However, the ensuing violence and loss of life in the "land of thc free and home of the brave" were certainly and undeniably regarded as criminal offenses that could be prosecuted in any court of law.

The line between brutality and freedom of expression and freedom of speech collided. Fear and apathy set in, most especially among the general public and those on the receiving end of unearned suffering. How do you function in a society where trust is speedily disappearing and interaction with people is absolutely on hold? The clarion call of Christ to "love your neighbor" is suddenly suppressed because evil is on the throne. It is difficult to tell, and frankly, humanity has no idea who "our neighbors" are anymore. People are not afraid to drag neighbors, friends, coworkers, and fellow members of the same society out in the middle of the night—drag them away from their loving and caring family, only to take away their freedom, steal their joy, and leave wives without their chosen loved ones. Children suddenly become fatherless, and loved ones are gone forever. The people who came to steal, to kill, and to destroy blatantly did so in the spirit of the Antichrist because they were the self-ordained rulers of the dark places of the world.

Those so-called Christians who could have become the light of the world, a unified voice of the oppressed, representing Christ at every level of human interaction, quickly signed up for witness protection instead and thereby became unwilling participants in the evil acts of the KKK. Nobody was bold enough to fight for those who could not fight for themselves, those who were suffering. The communities of African Americans became the communities of a bunch of "nobodies." Not only did they forget your name, but good deeds were forgotten, and many African Americans were forced to meet their makers by hangings and blatant destruction of what was once a thriving life.

Who wants to see their house firebombed or a loved one lynched in the middle of the night by those who are not afraid of anyone or any law? Expectations of violent reaction gave birth to a wide range of discrimination (in public and private places, in business, in government, etc.) against African Americans. It also gave birth to a whole gamut of psychological warfare designed to intimidate, demean, dehumanize, isolate, ignore, and outright reject their existence. Many African Americans were angry and extremely frustrated at what was going on in the hand of the people they thought were good neighbors and in the same society they helped build.

Many African Americans did not know how to handle what was happening. The carefully orchestrated psychological warfare against them was too emotionally and physically damaging. How do you go out and have fun in a society designed to refuse you? How do you handle words such as "Sir, you are not allowed to sit at the lunch counter," "You cannot use our restroom," "We simply cannot serve you here or provide services to you," or "We are not hiring anymore"? How do you function? As a parent, how do you tell your children, "I cannot stop at a restaurant to let you get a quick bite"? Forget about pride and dignity; they've been taken from you and are gone. You are basically reduced to the level of a nonperson—nobody, to be exact.

While the rest of America was busy acquiring land in record numbers, building skyscrapers, mansions, and huge businesses, while they were busy inventing and innovating, black people were forced to grapple with basically nothing. They were cornered, and most were forced to live in ghettos and barrios. Lack of education meant lack of dignity and lack of opportunities. Those with an education could not do much with it because of discrimination and limited opportunities. They were squeezed out only to fight, and for the most part kill one another, over crumbs.

If you cannot receive a dignified welcome and reception from any institution big or small, public or private, how do you think any person will react to you? Any type of interaction with European Americans—male or female—can quickly result in the display of fear, followed by an excessive reaction, such as shaking uncontrollably, in some cases with teary eyes. When police get involved, what kind of reaction do you expect in light of such captivating fear and the emotional reaction playing out in front of them?

Most police officers took the job intending to protect and to serve, regardless. They are supposed to be the only firewall between you and those who are not afraid to inflict pain (physical or psychological) on people without remorse. The law enforcement people are the only shield against violent attacks on members of any community. It is expected of them to be tough, but they are expected to be fair and follow what is just. However, many of them sided with evil and were not afraid to turn their backs against most African Americans. Many decided to exercise doubt when the truth was just not obvious. Many of them were not afraid to paint the disadvantaged as excessively angry and ready to inflict pain. By the same token, many of them were not afraid to follow the call of conscience, respect humanity, and treat everyone with respect.

When an encounter was between a black person and a white person in those days, and a police officer showed up, if the police officer was of a different skin color, the possibility of getting emotionally involved was enormously greater right from the moment the police officer walked in. If the African American person was slightly aggressive, the possibility of going out in shackles increased tremendously, because the officer was now emotionally involved. The African American person was probably angry because society had turned against them. Nobody was in their corner anymore. The police officer was probably going to be emotionally involved, thinking, *What if this was my mom, sister, or any member of my family?* The situation was now bound to escalate. The label of *angry black man* or *angry black woman* emerged. Society quickly became unkind and unreasonable, unwilling to understand the frustration of African Americans and the underlying reason for their anger. In any situation, the black person's unsolicited negative reaction quickly goes on display and usually leads to a baseless arrest and more ugly confrontations with the police.

The *angry black man* or *angry black woman* syndrome was unfair. How would you feel if your existence was threatened and your pride and joy were quickly evaporating before your eyes? No employer is willing to hire you. If you engage in a mediocre job and make a little income, you cannot treat yourself to a good meal in any restaurant. How would you feel if you were on a journey, and you are tired and weary but could not get accommodation in any hotel or motel because you are simply not welcome there? Educational ambition remains a dream that will never see the light of reality. Getting a place to live was impossible. Stores (any kind) were not welcoming and not ready to be kind to you. The neighborhood of black people quickly became the poorest neighborhood in town, and an average black person is the most uneducated and ignorant person who ever walked the face of the earth. You cannot get a loan to start a business because of the banks' stricter rules for the so-called black people. To say that black people were alienated is an understatement. They quickly became outcasts, rejected members of the human family. Evil took over and became the ruler of the free world.

To blame police officers for what they did not create is equally unfair. In the effort to maintain peace, law, and order in our confused and fear-stricken society, they too became unwilling participants in the ugly mess of discrimination and segregation. They cannot say to black people, "Go ahead and unleash your anger on people who may or may not have anything to do with the reason for your anger but are merely protecting their interests." To maintain peace, law, and order and still act fairly was just too challenging. They had to lean one way and let the judicial system decide. They are not always right. The question such as "Where did you get this expensive car you are driving?" or "Where did you get that good-looking and costly wristwatch?" are just too invading, too provoking, and too insulting to command respect and cooperation. The unsolicited advice of *shave your beard* or *cut that dreadlock off* or *appear cleaner next time* are too demeaning for many to handle.

Most police officers are basically good people. Their desire was to go out and perform their duties to protect and serve while maintaining order among the people. One of their expectations was to come home to their family, safe and sound. Like anybody, they too want to play an important role in the upbringing of their children. They want to spend quality time with their wives, girlfriends, or significant others and possibly go out on a romantic date when necessary. When they are faced with violent confrontation, not knowing what the other person might do, their reactions become unpredictable, depending on their training. There is no condoning of the taking of life when other and better options are available. By the same token, nothing justifies the loss of the life of a man or a woman whose job is to protect you and serve you as best as they know how.

After the civil war, evil took over, and we were left with hate, division, unnecessary suspicion, prejudice, and discrimination. The actions and inactions of so many individuals helped nurture and preserve it. At the top of the list of notable individuals in public positions in our generation is Governor George C. Wallace of Alabama, who once proclaimed, "Segregation now, segregation forever." There were hundreds and perhaps thousands of people in businesses and even Christian denominations who played major roles in prolonging the evil brought to life in 1865.

This act of inhumanity led to the unintentional description of which life matters. "Black lives matter" does not connote that the rest doesn't matter. It simply does not explicitly imply that. It means stop killing African Americans unnecessarily. Stop violating their rights, and stop treating them like nonpersons. Their lives matters. We need to take a deep breath to understand one another and look within for a better solution.

The Bible tells us about a ruler of the Jews by the name of Nicodemus. He went to Jesus, showering Him with praises in the effort to know what to do to inherit eternal life. What Jesus said to him was very confusing for his success, and the desire for wealth invaded his mind. It took him by surprise. Nicodemus asked Jesus for further explanation. Jesus did not provide him with a long list of things to do or not to do. He could have told him, at a minimum, thou shall not steal, thou shall not kill, and thou shall not destroy. Instead, Jesus simply said to Nicodemus, "Ye must be born again." There is no doubt we need transformation from within concerning our relationship with one another as members of the human family.

The solution to our division and the hate we are left with is not a choice between violence or nonviolence. The solution is in the fact that we need to see one another more positively, appreciate one another, and treat one another as equal without any negative, preconceived notions. We need to change our perceptions of one another, lift one another's spirit, and encourage one another. This is our choice: we must be born again. The time to stand up for what is right and reject, uproot, and destroy the seed of hate and division is now. There are so many men and women of goodwill who are not afraid to be coworkers with God to help change and destroy the platform of division forever.

STREAMS OF DIVISION

How did we end up where we are today, especially in this land of "we the people"? To recap the facts, some of us are here because of earlier natural displacement called the continental drift. Some are here because of individual or group exploration, personal ambition, or leadership's interest in discoveries and colonization that was never accurately reported. Finally, some are here against their will, and some are here voluntarily. Regardless of how or why, the reality is we are all here.

Attacking social evil in the interest of dismantling the platform of hate and division is not for the faint of heart. As difficult as it may seem, the goal of this book is to achieve that greater good through the presentation of facts to discredit the ugliness of the past. Solutions to the problem of this magnitude, handed over to us by those not afraid to disagree with God, necessitate that we take a careful look at the ugly problems of the past, including some psychological warfare still going on among us.

We need to begin to reject them one by one. The solution is not in a group effort but in each individual hand. The individual's role in the effort to dismantle the platform of hate and division requires unwavering effort and unmatched alignment with what is heavenly and godly, which is not easily available within groups. We have allowed so many selfish desires, inaccurate claims, assumptions, and unjust treatment of one another to divide us. To erase division, we need to look at what led us to where we are today and find our way out:

- The selfish desire of the people whose beginning we have no true history of, along with much unscientific research, conducted by people who are openly anti-God and designed to legitimize illegitimate claims of Caucasians, led humanity on a collision course with the will of God. The desire to outperform one another, along with the group or kingdom-inspired quest to be first, blinded the passionate and the noble side of humanity, thereby giving the stamp of approval to something totally selfish and in violation of divine law. Our never-ending ambition did not allow us to turn to one another but instead against one another. We allowed greed and covetousness to drive a wedge and a deep divide. The better-than-you attitude of many did not help.

- In the individual effort to be right, some pushed to have their names carved in stone forever and took advantage of the chaos brought about as a result of selfish and isolating claims. As a result, they created fictional history deeply rooted and grounded in greed, misnomers, and more false claims without regard for others and for truth. Much of the erroneous history that came out of the self-glorified ambitions of the past seriously insults intelligence in every way. Some people were credited and showered with unearned accolades and praises, while others were deliberately ignored and marginalized. Dreams were intentionally shattered. Many people were selfishly ignored, and their pride—as well as that of their people and nation—was trampled. We fought one another over individual land ownership. The weak did not have anything to show for their effort, which gave way to a huge disregard for unity. The greatest misnomer ever in the history of humankind—which is the delineation of different races—was never looked into, dissected, and debated but ignorantly accepted. They looked at those who are at a greater disadvantage and simply came to the unfounded conclusion that these people could not possibly be the same as us.
- There should be no credible platform or place in any society for divisive and destructive studies by anyone or any group of people designed to pin one ethnic group against another.

Superiority exists only in the mind and the eyes of the beholder, with no basis in fact and no justification in reality. Some people are just naturally devoid of conscience and arrogantly blind to the feelings of others. Being privileged with higher education does not provide anyone or any group of people an instrument to destroy pride, hope, and aspirations of fellow human beings. We are all God's children entitled to enjoy the goodness of the Lord in the land of the living.

- Dangerous and twisted history in the hands of some twisted minds called professors is as dangerous as the weapons of mass destruction. To be passionate about what you know to be true is one thing, but to be passionate about something you are not even sure as to how it came about along, with lots of covered underlying facts about it, is another thing. Some people talk about history as if to say they were actually there when it happened. If you go against their twisted version, you can be sure you are going to leave that class with a failing grade. In that case, lies and inaccuracies become the new norms, and truth is forever on the scaffold, with wrong forever on the throne. When people are turned against one another, we expect our law enforcement officers to come and clean up the mess, fixing the problems. What a stretch in expectation and extreme deviation from the call of duty.
- In a time of ideological and political differences, which led to the emergence of the Cold War, they did not hesitate to create a new label such as *third world,* which is derogatory and demeaning, to put it mildly. Alignment or nonalignment with the North Atlantic Treaty Organization popularly known as NATO or the Communist Bloc during the Cold War was the reason nations in Africa were labeled as third world. Why should the discord between different ethnic groups in Europe define the rest of the world? "The United States, Western European nations, and their allies represented the First World," while the Soviet Union, China, Cuba, and their allies represented the Second World. Africa, which was never involved in the feud, received

the label of "third world" which carries negative connotations, while, in fact, some nations in Africa were democratic, and some were communist or socialist. For anyone to say that "I am from a third world country" is like saying "I am from a poor and underdeveloped country," which creates more division.

- Herbal remedies in Africa are looked upon as evil, voodoo, black magic, or witchcraft. In Europe, Asia, and anywhere else around the world, a healing element is embraced as what it is—herbal remedy. There is nothing in history or in Christianity to suggest that herbal remedies of one ethnic group are better than the herbal remedies of another ethnic group. We all know about the question of Jeremiah when he noticed the declined health of his people: "Is there no balm in Gilead, is there no physician there?" Christoph Meiners's label of "beautiful White race" and the "ugly Black race" helped permanently solidify this unspeakable hate and division.
- Ask anyone to draw a picture of the devil as they imagine him to be, and you will see various drawings of a black person with red horns on his forehead, a weird and gross-looking face, and teeth hanging out. The perceived image of the devil called Lucifer is in sharp contrast to how God described him in scriptures. As pointed out earlier, he was called the morning star, and his image as portrayed in the scripture is one of outstanding beauty and talent. He epitomized everything pleasantly and was admirably beautiful. All these characteristics led to his downfall, with the desire to make himself greater than or superior to God. That kind of makes you wonder at to the validity of and the motive behind Meiners's assumption.
- Africans involved in innovation of any kind in technology or medicine is unimaginable. If the so-called black man develops a piece of technology, the question on the mind of most people is "How?" Not only that. If he is not ignored by all sponsors, he will soon pack up for lack of attention and coverage from the media, which was provided to other founders and inventors like him, who are not African Americans. You can put out as many

press releases as possible; as soon as the media discovers that you are an African American, the willful and intentional effort to ignore you is going to spread like an inferno. The fact that they provide coverage to one African American in ten thousand is more than enough. Once coverage is denied, you are doomed. Other African Americans will ignore you, ridicule you, and at times laugh at you and your effort. Your friends will stay away, thinking there is something wrong with you—until they too begin to experience similar discriminations and abandonment.

- There are still some individuals who simply cannot picture African Americans in luxuries, even in 2019. The fact that you are a successful businessperson does not usually translate into respect. You might get some occasional *wow,* but the truth is most people believe you are one of the few beneficiaries of government handouts. In reality, most people believe that they are far better than you, know more than you, and, as a result, can perform better than you if given the same chance.
- Look up the word *black* in the dictionary, and you will see things such as "devoid of light, full of anger, clandestine, hopeless, dirty, seriously bad or unfortunate, dishonorable, evil, and bruised eye." In some countries, the phrase *black face* is another word for a sad face, an unhappy mood, or an angry look. The word *white* is described as pure, pleasant, incandescent, and everything opposite of black. A white lie is far better and acceptable. Does connection to Meiners's assumption ring a bell?
- Lack of opportunities can make a genius look stupid and incompetent. If the cloud of doubt, inferiority complex, and lack of support—financial and otherwise—do not kill you and your dreams or destroy your hope, isolation will. Whether we are ready to admit it or not, we all become participants in the evil acts of hate, prejudice, and discrimination, created for us by people whose goal was to destroy. The fact that some privileged individuals managed to carefully recreate and repackage hate and discrimination makes it more like it is the victims' problem. Nonchalant attitudes from the general public can be incredibly

discouraging. In the words of Martin Luther King Jr., "Our generation will have to repent not only for the acts and words of the children of darkness but also for the fears and apathy of the children of light."

- "I demand justice" sounds great and plausible, but from African Americans, these are strange words. How can you demand justice within a system that believes you are guilty until proven innocent? Some laws are written to cast doubt, depending on who you are, while some laws are written to guide in the administration of justice. Some judges are already under the preconceived notion and understanding as to who the criminals are or what they look like, while a lot of judges are willing to look at facts to determine which way the pendulum of justice swings. Some judges treat everyone the same because of their deep belief in doing unto others as they would want others to do unto them, but some are outright ignorant and impossible.
- How do you successfully function in a world made to recognize the expertise of your colleagues who happen to be members of the only privileged group, and you are despised, ignored, marginalized, or treated with doubt and dismay? Without regard for your feelings, the desire to continue to discredit you by those waiting in line to shine or receive full credit at your expense is a never-ending desire.
- Incarceration was expected to serve as a deterrent to crimes. However, that is not practically and realistically true. Incarceration due to petty crimes, as opposed to rehabilitation, becomes a stepping-stone to greater crime. Prison by itself is nothing more than institutional entrapment for the training and production of more potential criminals. It is also a recruiting ground for extremists of every kind. A lot of innocent people are imprisoned for crimes they did not commit, while many are given maximum sentencing for crimes other people received warnings and scolding for. Prison is nothing more than just another instrument of hate, division, discrimination, and

extreme prejudice. Its population does not reflect reality but a shameful conclusion of our judicial system.

- African Americans are not innocent in the nurturing of all negativities currently existing in the society against them. For some unknown reasons, they are hanging on and refuse to let go of the memories of slavery, as if to say we were the only ethnic group ever affected by it. We make it easy for prejudice, low expectation of us, and many inequalities to continue. How can you constantly refer to your own existence by one catastrophic shameful event of the past to the exclusive neglect of all positive contributions made by many? Go back to ancient times and see the shameful stories of slavery everywhere.
  - o The Irish and many other Europeans and Asians were held in slavery here in the United States as well as in many other places on the continent of America. The fact, supported by laws and other records, remains undeniable. As revealed by appendix 1, 2(a) and 2(b), references to slaves are explicit, as are references to free persons. Here in the United States and elsewhere in America, indentured servants or chattel slaves (especially chattel slaves) are not allowed to buy or sell any other person as a slave. The right to buy or sell anyone was only available to those who were here as free men and women. No matter how you slice it, if any European can be bought or sold, that qualifies as slaves. Not only that, Africans were once allowed, prior to 1705, to buy and sell Europeans held as slaves (slaves that were not Africans), which constitutes them as masters and owners of those Europeans held as slaves.
  - o "Nigro" does not mean slaves but is the Spanish word for "black." Europeans who came here as servants and slaves were openly sold and bought by free people (including free Africans) prior to 1705. This fact prompted the law to be reprinted, hereby revealed as appendix 1. Historians intentionally changed the truth, thereby developing a misnomer of high proportions. However, you will never

hear any other ethnic group referring to their own existence with phrases such as *since slavery*. They refuse to let slavery define them. If anything, they would like to deny it ever happened. In the eyes of many African Americans, slavery is African American history and something exclusive to them. No one knows or remembers that before explorations, Africans were here. A lot are not aware of the fact that before Christopher Columbus, we were here, and before the Pilgrims landed in Plymouth, we were here. We came here as warriors, explorers, and adventurers. Slavery did not come until later—1619 to be exact.

- We call each other *nigger* and joke openly about this dehumanizing word as if to say that this is really funny and "I like it!" We have become so immune and desensitized to the expectation of human dignity that we cannot see what is good in one another. We embrace meager living and poverty with so much joy and pride. Those hardworking people who are making it among us are constantly being referred to by the rest as *rich nigger*. When society looks down or treats the best of us with insult, neglect, and disdain, we help them find a way to blame the victim and justify the deplorable actions of society. No one is as mean to African Americans as African Americans.
- We are not afraid to kill one another over something so minute, something so infinitesimal, something so unworthy of the loss of life! African Americans are so unappreciative of such immensely talented, highly intelligent, and creative minds among them. Yet we expect society to be respectful, appreciative, kind, lovingly inclusive, and eager to grant equal opportunities. You should not expect from others what you are not willing to plant and nurture in your own communities. The time to turn to one another and not on one another is now.
- There are so many churches in black neighborhoods, you would think you are in the Vatican. Yet the most obvious and thriving businesses in black neighborhoods are funeral homes. Drugs are more important and precious than human lives. Money, which

we do not know how to invest, is dearer than the lives of our fellow brothers and sisters. If a girl should give an indication of a breakup, the possibility of finding her and her new lover dead is extremely high. If the Savior was standing in the midst of many African Americans, His clarion call would, no doubt, include "African Americans, you must be born again."

The solution to what we are grappling with is not to create new problems. It is not to turning against one another. It is not to retaliate a blow with a blow. It is not in the endless argument of who is right or wrong. The solution to the problem of division is standing up against hate, against division, against injustice, against prejudice, and against religious intolerance and discrimination. If ever there was a time to say to everyone in the United States and the world, "You must be born again," now is the time.

We inherited a multitude of problems. Are we expecting law enforcement people to find solutions? No doubt there are some rotten eggs among them. Needless to say, the first part of the officer's job is to make sure evil does not prevail in our society. In that way, they have to protect. I hope they believe this. The second part is to serve you by apprehending threats (not eliminating threats) through proper implementation of the rule of law, thereby allowing justice to have the last say. Do not forget that if they are under a different mind-set or with prejudicial and dangerous assumptions not rooted and grounded in fact and reality, they might take the law into their own hands in a split second. Many of them understand that they are not above the law and could be subject to the same harsh reality they swore to protect the public from. The fact that they are licensed to carry weapons makes some forget about their duties to society.

PATHWAY TO PEACEFUL COEXISTENCE

The road to peaceful coexistence is marred with selfishness, inaccuracies, and twisted history, resulting in misinformation meant to destroy hope and pride rather than encourage them. We deliberately or inadvertently put ourselves on an impossible journey, not realizing the magnitude of the destruction that lies ahead. We (society) intentionally throw people into an impossible darkness and expect them to find their way out. We are the architects of the destructive division currently in our midst. Many of us, through fear and apathy, became a willing or, in some cases, passive participant in the nurturing, longevity, and sustainability of the evil act of division, organized and supported by twisted science and forcefully implemented by those of evil intent, handed down to many innocent generations.

Some of us might be thinking that it is too late to roll back the hand of time. I have to disagree. We can start to set the record straight while making attempts to take a detour to peaceful living, in the interest of finding an end to division. If we allow division to continue, it will never cease, leading to more division. If we continue to allow negative or inferior expectations of people to continue, subsequent anger and resentment will never end. If we allow prejudice and discrimination to continue, having the last say in reality, trust and empathy could vanish forever. If we stop allowing other people the opportunity to be productive members of society, our generation will be the beneficiary of our inaction. If we fail to allow people to love unconditionally and permanently, without injecting our uninvited objection, misery, regret, and sadness, unsolicited suffering will continue to invade the minds of many of our loved ones. If we shut the door to opportunities because of our biased and twisted preferences, we will, no doubt, continue to contribute to the imperfection of a society highly insensitive to the feeling of others. We have a choice to be coworkers with God or continue to maintain hearts of stone, always looking for a way to rationalize our actions without attention to the divine call to action. Repentance is about turning away from everything ungodly, sinful, and evil to do the will of God.

Refusing to cooperate with evil is always a brave, noble, and divine thing to do. Conscientious objectors on the wrong side of social justice are nothing but rabble-rousers. A creative approach in the interest of peaceful coexistence is what this chapter is all about. The time to help those people-loving law enforcement officers resume the role they signed up for is now. Those open-minded and God-fearing law enforcement officers did not sign up to be hated members of the society they swore to protect and serve. They cannot be left alone to deal with the fear, anger, prejudice, and resentment in our society. The general public needs to step in; financial institutions, the media, and the government cannot stand on the sidelines hoping to one day get a favorable outcome.

The quest for solutions requires a U-turn back to selfless, encouraging, and sound interpersonal relationships with people everywhere. To continue on the road to nowhere in search of a better way to help humanity is unwise. It is also profound evidence of a defective mind. This is not the time to insist upon an arrogant frame of mind, thinking we are the only one with the answer, without consideration of other inputs. The problem of division is bigger than we can ever imagine and is equally deadly. However, the road to peaceful unification starts with baby steps. Needless to say, we cannot go back to more than 250 years ago to try to undo the evil orchestrated and planted in our society, but we can gently, without resistance, embrace a different path in the interest of peaceful coexistence. Cooperation from everyone is a must, and there is simply no other way to approach it.

The clarion call on different members of society as suggested here is in no way exhaustive and does not exclude any other way equally as good or better. What I recommend here are in the words of President

Abraham Lincoln, "With malice toward none, with charity for all, with firmness in the right as God gives us to see the right, let us strive on to finish the work we are in, to bind up the nation's wounds, to care for him who shall have borne the battle and for his widow and his orphan, to do all which may achieve and cherish a just and lasting peace among ourselves and with all nations." We all have parts to play. Please find yours and let us bind together to eliminate division:

a) *Parents and legal guardians' responsibilities.* Parents of little children are in the front row of all required action necessary to eliminate hate, prejudice, and division, including discrimination and injustice. We need to help our children understand the following:
   i. Meaning of inclusiveness and tolerance regardless of differences, regardless of ethnicity, and regardless of skin color.
   ii. The need to respect lives and that we can agree to disagree without having to shoot anyone.
   iii. The importance of the fact that all lives matters. We are all precious in God's sight.
   iv. The value of respect for others.
   v. We need to treat others like they would like to be treated.
   vi. The fact that division as currently exists among humanity is not scriptural and not encouraged or commanded by God.
b) *Expected contributions from educators.* Teachers from kindergarten to high school need to help children understand what stepping into the other person's shoes means, what it means to reach out to others without expecting anything in return, and what it means to make life worth living for all.
   i. Our children need to establish sound relationships with law enforcement officers without expecting unhealthy rites of passage and excuses for wrongdoings. They need a way to eliminate fear and discrimination toward those in uniform.
   ii. Children need to understand the important role those who are sworn to protect us play in our society.
   iii. They need to understand public safety and the link between law enforcement officers and public safety.

iv. They also need to understand what respect for authority means. Children need to know that the law enforcement people are parents too. They are also sons and daughters of a loving parent(s), brothers and sisters of caring relatives, and boyfriends, girlfriends, husbands, and wives of loving and caring people.

v. It is advisable for pre-K and kindergarten teachers to include occasional trips to police precincts to allow children to get to meet and know those who are in public service in the interest of public safety.

vi. It is important to impress upon them what togetherness and respect for one another means. Division of any kind can have no place in our society; every life matters.

c) *Training for law enforcement people.* In a world full of people from different ethnic backgrounds and cultural differences, respect and cultural sensitivity are expected without deviating from the call of duty. Training designed for law enforcement people must include the following:

i. Appearance is not an indicator of criminality.

ii. A teenage child in a hoody does not mean that the child is up to no good and should be treated with disdain.

iii. A person running away from a law enforcement officer should be stopped, arrested, and prosecuted when necessary but not killed.

iv. A person sitting quietly in his or her car with a registered firearm when pulled over by a police officer should not be killed. Paranoia is highly destructive.

v. There is a better way to get another human being out of his or her car with their hands up without shooting.

vi. There is no need to shoot another human being (one of the people you swore to protect and serve) so many times to get their attention. What would it take to realize that after two or three bullets, this person might not be going home to their loved ones? There is no law against the following:

a) Being a moron

b) Acting stupid

vii. Rewarding a police officer accused of a crime with paid leave insults intelligence and is a slap in the face of democracy and law and order.

viii. Sparing the lives of people of the same skin color as you are and eliminating the lives of those who are different and outside of your ethnic group is not only morally wrong and sinful, it is antihuman and against everything godly. No matter what we think or believe, the Most High will always rule in the kingdom of humans.

ix. Leaving everything to an individual law enforcement officer's judgment without some legal guidance or adequate training is too dangerous.

x. Practicing shooting in a shooting range using an avatar or something depicting a member of a specific ethnic group with a specific color of skin should be discouraged and no longer allowed. It is designed to contribute to the existing psychological warfare and hate among us, and it can greatly and psychologically affect thinking within that split second you have to make a decision.

xi. Make sure any suspect is out of their vehicle with hands up and free of any object. If you notice or think you see anything suspicious, learn how to shoot the object out of the suspect's hand(s) to make an arrest.

xii. Encourage law enforcement officers to embrace a pre-K or kindergarten student of a different color skin to help guide and lead them in the right path. Also, they should occasionally visit the child to be sure the child does not deviate from what is right.

d) *Responsibility of law enforcement people.* The training and job descriptions of law enforcement officers do not say that you are above the law. The neighborhood of a different ethnic group should not be misconstrued as going into the wild. Civility means respecting what is good and encouraging the best in us all. Reality tells us the following:

i. People are not born criminals.

ii. Anyone can fall into the wrong crowd, thereby acquiring bad behaviors and forgetting home-instilled behaviors.

iii. Children can exhibit defiant behaviors depending on the circumstances, and it does not always translate into resentment toward law enforcement and definitely not toward anyone in particular.

iv. Refusing to obey an order at the very first command could be due to having a shocking reaction to what is going on and is not necessarily a sign of disobedience.

v. To err is human. We will not be able to wipe out crime and stop criminals among us. It is good to make arrests and let justice prevail.

e) *The general public.* Responding to a simple question from God of "Where is your brother?" Cain came up with another question, asking God, "Am I my brother's keeper?" Most of what we think we know about one another is dreadfully flawed. To intentionally twist history in favor of elevating one ethnic group to the extreme decimation of another ethnic group is appalling. To make one ethnic group the bearer and scapegoat of the shameful event of the past is immoral. It is equally immoral that the victims will not cease defining themselves by slavery—something not worthy of remembrance. References such as *the sons of former slaves* and *the sons of former slave owners* cut across ethnicity. We all have our respective share in not letting go of the shameful history of the past. The fact that there were many African American slave owners as well as white slave owners is enough to make African Americans reject any future references to slavery. It is not exclusive to African Americans. This is necessary and something that we need to do in the interest of healthy interactions and the pride of future generations. If ever there was one more march to organize, it is the march to erase the ugly history of the past.

f) We are on this journey together and cannot afford to leave anyone behind. Personal ambition and the desire to excel or to be first is healthy and required for growth. To fight for it is human, but to kill for it is against divine law, constitutional law, and moral law. It is always good to know that the only way to secure your rightful place in reality is to let other people shine as well.

i. The need for mutual respect cannot be over emphasized: respect others.
ii. Treat people like you would like to be treated.
iii. Try not to be too quick to judge or condemn; looks can be deceiving.

g) *Government's role.* In the land of the free and home of the brave, expecting the right of all to be protected is not asking for too much. In the land of "we the people," the government needs to make sure the right to reach your potential, to grow, to positively contribute to society, and to reject insult and evil through the civil act of protesting for right are protected and not infringed upon. Democracy and the Christian values adopted by the founding fathers nee dot be able to continue to thrive and not be trampled upon. We cannot afford not to encourage the following:
i. Equal protection under the law
ii. Civil rights
iii. Justice for all (the judicial system needs to understand that detaining people longer than necessary because of the color of their skin is inhuman)
iv. Freedom from oppression
v. Opportunity to blossom

h) It is the government's responsibility, as well as the responsibility of the media, to help erase all existing misnomers and misinformation about the human race. We do not have different races but one race—the human race. It is equally the responsibility of the government and the media to let the general public know the truth about how we got to where we are today, through natural displacement and exploration, without building on the wrong and dehumanizing information from the past.

i) *Financial institutions.* Providing financial opportunities to people based on the color of their skin is morally wrong and shameful. Evaluation of business plans to provide financial support should not result in a never-ending, doubtful request for more information designed to dehumanize, insult intelligence, and eventually kill hopes and dreams all because of the fact that they are different from you. In a quote usually attributed to Abraham Lincoln, the author Rev. William John Henry Boetcker wrote, "You cannot bring about prosperity by discouraging thrift. You cannot strengthen the weak by weakening the strong. You cannot help the wage earner by pulling down the wage payer. You cannot further the brotherhood of man by encouraging class hatred. You cannot help the poor by destroying the rich. You cannot build character and courage by taking away man's initiative and independence. You cannot help men permanently by doing for them what they could and should do for themselves."

j) *The media.* You are at the forefront of the dissemination of information, and you are also at the forefront of misinformation and misnomers. You (the media) are not unaware of the truth about the human race, but you continuc on an unhealthy path to more division. Referring to a nation as a race is not only wrong, it is unhealthy and poor nutrition for the minds of men and women everywhere. You are not unaware of what is true, but for some unknown reason, you allow misinformation and misnomers to go on uncorrected. It is difficult to figure out if your action is deliberate and intentional in the interest of creating conflict to increase ratings or something more sinister and destructive. The focus of the media is increasing the pride of one ethnic group over the rest. It appears they are not friends of equal coverage or equal opportunity. They are the kingmaker of only one ethnic group and not for the human race.

Variety is good because God is good—different shades (color and creed), different sizes, height, and other characteristics. We speak different languages and fall into different cultures. This is what *godly* looks like. What you see each day you are outside of your habitat and ethnicity and what you see on the street are the true, unmistaken images of God as described in scriptures. If you want to disagree, do not hold back. Jesus, the only begotten Son of God, is coming back again, and we are not sure what His appearance will be. In the book of 1 John 3:2, the Bible says, "Beloved, now are we the sons of God, and it doth not yet appear what we shall be: but we know that, when he shall appear, we shall be like him; for we shall see him as he is."

AUTHOR'S NOTE

The appendixes provided (which are copies of the law of 1705) in addition to the outcome of the census received from the Census Bureau are meant to be eye-opening. They are provided for the sole purpose of educating the minds of many, to destroy inequalities, hate, and division. They are not meant to establish a new superiority but equal rights.

It is not uncommon to live for many years under the illusion of false superiority. It is not uncommon to think highly of yourself while neglecting those who are equally good. In the words of John Donne, "No man is an island entire of itself."

APPENDIX 1

October 1705-CHAP. XLIX. An act concerning Servants and Slaves. Obtained with the help of the Library of Congress.

AUTHOR'S NOTE

This statute included a definition of who would became a slave upon entering Virginia and repeated previous restrictions placed upon enslaved persons in addition to new constraints. The law contained some modifications on the punishments placed on white women who bore a mulatto child and white individuals who married a person of color in 1691. The legislators made it clear that Christianity was not the path to freedom for a slave.

Please understand the following:

- This was a bill, introduced, passed, and signed into law back in 1705. This was the actual law in the state of Virginia.
- No law was ever passed based on speculation or to correct something that was never considered a problem.

Read it very carefully, and you will find the truth about slavery and references to both "white" slaves as well as "black" or "negro" slaves, including other slaves of another ethnic group. In addition to the law hereby revealed, please read my notes calling attention to some sections within the law.

Read it very carefully, and you will find the truth about slavery and references to both "white" slaves as well as "black" or "negro" slaves, including other slaves of another ethnic group. In addition to the law hereby revealed, please read my notes calling attention to some sections within the law.

How this and other historical documents about the fact were intentionally ignored by many who deliberately made slavery the history of black people exclusively defies logic. How did African Americans become the bearers of something so demeaning and dehumanizing, a stain on dignity, while others are proudly and boldly claiming something that belongs to us all—the United States of America?

I. And also be it enacted, by the authority aforesaid, and it is hereby enacted, That all servants imported and brought into this country, by sea or land, who were not christians in their native country, (except Turks and Moors in amity with her majesty, and others that can make due proof their being free in England, or any other christian country, before they were shipped, in order to transportation hither (shall be accounted and be slaves, and as such be here bought and sold notwithstanding a conversion to christianity afterwards.

II. And be it enacted, by the authority aforesaid, and it is hereby enacted, That *if_any person or persons shall hereafter import into this colony, and here sell as a slave, any person or persons that shall have been a freeman in any christian country, island, or plantation,* such importer and seller as aforesaid, shall forfeit and pay, to the party from who the said freeman shall recover his freedom, double the sum for which the said freeman was sold. To be recovered, in any court of record within this colony, according to the course of the common law, wherein the defendant shall not be admitted to plead in bar, any act or statute for limitation of actions.

III. Provided always, That a slave's being in England, shall not be sufficient to discharge him of his slavery, without other proof of his being manumitted there.

IV. And for a further christian care and usage of all christian servants, *Be it also enacted, by the authority aforesaid, and it is hereby enacted, That no negros, mulattos, or Indians, although christians, or Jews, Moors, Mahometans, or other infidels, shall, at any time, purchase any christian servant, nor any other, except of their own complexion, or such as are declared slaves by this act*: And if any negro, mulatto, or Indian, Jew, Moor, Mahometan, or other infidel, or such as are declared slaves by this act, shall, notwithstanding, purchase any christian white servant, the said servant shall, ipso facto, become free and acquit from any service then due, and shall be so held, deemed, and taken: And if any person, having such christian servant, shall intermarry with any such negro, mulatto, or Indian, Jew, Moor, Mahometan, or other infidel, every christian white servant of every such person so intermarrying, shall, ipso facto, become free and acquit from any service then due to such master or mistress so intermarrying, as aforesaid.

V. And also be it enacted, by the authority aforesaid, and it is hereby enacted, That no person whatsoever shall, buy, sell, or receive of, to, or from, any servant, or slave, any coin or commodity whatsoever, without the leave, licence, or consent of the master or owner of the said servant, or slave: And if any person shall, contrary hereunto, without the leave or licence aforesaid, deal with any servant, or slave, he or she so offending, shall be imprisoned one calender month, without bail or main-prize; and then, also continue in prison, until he or she shall find good security, in the sum of ten pounds current money of Virginia, for the good behaviour for one year following; wherein, a second offence shall be a breach of the bond; and moreover shall forfeit and pay four times the value of the things so bought, sold, or received, to the master or owner of such servant, or slave: To be recovered, with costs, by action upon the case, in any court of record in this her majesty's colony and dominion, wherein no essoin, protection, or wager of law, or other than one imparlance, shall be allowed.

AUTHOR'S NOTE

Italics in paragraphs V and XI are mine. I have to call attention to the following:

> That if any person or persons shall hereafter import into this colony, and here sell as a slave, any person or persons that shall have been a freeman in any christian country, island, or plantation …

Any "Christian country" in paragraph V is mainly referring to countries in Europe because the people of African countries in those days were regarded as infidels. Also "Island" is specifically mentioned. The phrase "here sell as slave" is without a doubt in reference to European slaves. It does not matter how historians would like to interpret this or turn it around. The fact is hereby established that slaves were brought to this part of the world from different continents and countries. The nineteen Africans brought to Charleston in Virginia were not the only ones, and the blemish of slavery cannot be exclusively pinned on Africans.

Regardless of any classification later assigned by those who would like to talk about history that is historically false, "servants" and "slaves" are basically the same. The act of buying and selling another human being constitutes and meets the undeniable definition of slavery. No single ethnic group should have to bear the shameful and demeaning burden of the label of slavery while others enjoy a false sense of superiority with audacity, loudly claiming that this is their land.

> VI. Provided always, and be it enacted, That when any person or persons convict for dealing with a servant, or slave, contrary to this act, shall not immediately give good and sufficient security for his or her good behaviour, as aforesaid: then in such case, the court shall order thirty-nine lashes, well laid on, upon the bare back of such offender, at the common whipping-post of the county, and the said offender to be thence discharged of giving such bond and security.

VII. And if any woman servant shall have a bastard child by a negro, or mulatto, over and above the years service due to her master or owner, she shall immediately, upon the expiration of her time to her then present master or owner, pay down to the church-wardens of the parish wherein such child shall be born, for the use of the said parish, fifteen pounds current money of Virginia, or be by them sold for five years, to the use aforesaid: And if a free christian white woman shall have such bastard child, by a negro, or mulatto, for every such offence, she shall, within one month after her delivery of such bastard child, pay to the church-wardens for the time being, of the parish wherein such child shall be born, for the use of the said parish fifteen pounds current money of Virginia, or be by them sold for five years to the use aforesaid: And in both the said cases, the church-wardens shall bind the said child to be a servant, until it shall be of thirty one years of age.

VIII. And for a further prevention of that abominable mixture and spurious issue, which hereafter may increase in this her majesty's colony and dominion, as well by English, and other white men and women intermarrying with negroes or mulattos, as by their unlawful coition with them, Be it enacted, by the authority aforesaid, and it is hereby enacted, *That whatsoever English, or other white man or woman, being free, shall intermarry with a negro or mulatto man or woman, bond or free,* shall, by judgment of the county court, be committed to prison, and there remain, during the space of six months, without bail or mainprize; and shall forfeit and pay ten pounds current money of Virginia, to the use of the parish, as aforesaid.

AUTHOR'S NOTE

The italics in paragraph XIX are mine. I just have to call your attention to this phrase: "That whatsoever English, or other white man or woman, being free." "Being free" is specifically mentioned here for a reason. In the interest of clarity, please understand that not all "English or other 'white'" men and women came here as free men and women. If they all did, there would be no reason to reemphasize what was widely known and obvious.

IX. And be it further enacted, That no minister of the church of England, or other minister, or person whatsoever, within this colony and dominion, shall hereafter wittingly presume to marry a white man with a negro or mulatto woman; or to marry a white woman with a negro or mulatto man, upon pain of forfeiting and paying, for every such marriage the sum of ten thousand pounds of tobacco; one half to our sovereign lady the Queen, her heirs and successors, for and towards the support of the government, and the contingent charges thereof; and the other half to the informer; To be recovered, with costs, by action of debt, bill, plaint, or information, in any court of record within this her majesty's colony and dominion, wherein no essoin, protection, or wager of law, shall be allowed.

X. And for encouragement of all persons to take up runaways, Be it enacted, by the authority aforesaid, and it is hereby enacted, That for the taking up of every servant, or slave, if ten miles, or above, from the house or quarter where such servant, or slave was kept, there shall be allowed by the public, as a reward to the taker-up, two hundred pounds of tobacco; and if above five miles, and under ten, one hundred pounds of tobacco: Which said several rewards of two hundred, and one hundred pounds of tobacco, shall also be paid in the county where such taker-up shall reside, and shall be again levied by the public upon the master or ownmer of such runaway, for re-imbursement of the public, every justice of the peace before whom such runaway shall be brought, upon the taking up, shall mention the proper-name and sur-name of the taker-up, and the county of his or her residence, together with the time and place of taking up the said runaway; and shall also mention the name of the said runaway, and the proper-name and sur-name of the master or owner of such runaway, and the county of his or her residence, together with the distance of miles, in the said justice's judgment, from the place of taking up the said runaway, to the house or quarter where such runaway was kept.

XI. Provided, That when any negro, or other runaway, that doth not speak English, and cannot, or through obstinacy will not, declare the name of his or her masters or owner, that then it shall be sufficient for the said justice to certify the same, instead of the name of such runaway, and the proper name and sur-name of his or her master or owner, and the county of his or her residence and distance of miles, as aforesaid; and in such case, shall, by his warrant, order the said runaway to be conveyed to the public gaol, of this country, there to be continued prisoner until the master or owner shall be known; who, upon paying the charges of the imprisonment, or giving caution to the prison-keeper for the same, together with the reward of two hundred or one hundred pounds of tobacco, as the case shall be, shall have the said runaway restored.

XII. And further, the said justice of the peace, when such runaway shall be brought before him, shall, by his warrant commit the said runaway to the next constable, and therein also order him to give the said runaway so many lashes as the said justice shall think fit, not exceeding the number of thirty-nine; and then to be conveyed from constable to constable, until the said runaway shall be carried home, or to the country gaol, as aforesaid, every constable through whose hands the said runaway shall pass, giving a receipt at the delivery; and every constable failing to execute such warrant according to the tenor thereof, or refusing to give such receipt, shall forefeit and pay two hundred pounds of tobacco to the church-wardens of the parish wherein such failure shall be, for the use of the poor of the said parish: To be recovered, with costs, by action of debt, in any court of record in this her majesty's colony and dominion, wherein no essoin, protection or wager of law, shall be allowed. And such corporal punishment shall not deprive the master or owner of such runaway of the other satisfaction here in this act appointed to be made upon such servant's running away.

XIII. And be it enacted, by the authority aforesaid, and it is hereby enacted, That if any constable, or sheriff, into whose hands a runaway servant or slave shall be committed, by virtue of this act, shall suffer such runaway to escape, the said constable or sheriff shall be liable to the action of the party agrieved, for recovery of his damages, at the common law with costs.

XIV. And also be it enacted, by the authority aforesaid, and it is hereby enacted, That no master, mistress, or overseer of a family, shall knowingly permit any slave, not belonging to him or her, to be and remain upon his or her plantation, above four hours at any one time, without the leave of such slave's master, mistress, or overseer, on penalty of one hundred and fifty pounds of tobacco to the informer; cognizable by a justice of the peace of the county wherein such offence shall be committed.

XV. And if any slave resist his master, or owner, or other person, by his or her order, correcting such slave, and shall happen to be killed in such correction, it shall not be accounted felony; but the master, owner, and every such other person so giving correction, shall be free and acquit of all punishment and accusation for the same, as if such incident had never happened: And also, if any negro, mulatto, or Indian, bond or free, shall at any time, lift his or her hand, in opposition against any christian, not being negro, mulatto, or Indian, he or she so offending shall, for every such offence, proved by the oath of the party, receive on his or her bare back, thirty lashes, well laid on; cognizable by a justice of the peace for that county wherein such offence shall be committed.

XVI. And also be it enacted, by the authority aforesaid, and it is hereby enacted, That no slave go armed with gun, sword, club, staff, or other weapon, nor go from off the plantation and seat of land where such slave shall be appointed to live, without a certificate of leave in writing, for so doing, from his or her master, mistress, or overseer: And if any slave shall be found offending herein, it shall be lawful for any person or persons to apprehend and deliver such slave to the next constable or head-borough, who is hereby enjoined and required, without further order or warrant, to give such slave twenty lashes on his or her bare back well laid on, and so send him or her home: And all horses, cattle, and hogs, now belonging, or that hereafter shall belong to any slave, or of any slaves mark in this her majesty's colony and dominion, shall be seised and sold by the church-wardens of the parish, wherein such horses, cattle, or hogs shall be, and the profit thereof applied to the use of the poor of the said parish: And also, if any damage shall be hereafter committed by any slave living at a quarter where there is no christian overseer, the master or owner of such slave shall be liable to action for the trespass and damage, as if the same had been done by him or herself.

XVII. And also it is hereby enacted and declared, That baptism of slaves doth not exempt them from bondage; and that all children shall be bond or free, according to the condition of their mothers, and the particular direction of this act.

XVIII. And whereas, many times, slaves run away and lie out, hid or lurking in swamps, woods, and other obscure places, killing hogs, and committing other injuries to the inhabitants of this her majesty's colony and dominion, Be it therefore enacted, by the authority aforesaid, and it is hereby enacted, That in all such cases, upon intelligence given of any slaves lying out, as aforesaid, any two justices (Quorum unus) of the peace of the county wherein such slave is supposed to lurk or do mischief, shall be and are impowered and required to issue proclamation against all such slaves, reciting their names, and owners names, if they are known, and thereby requiring them, and every of them, forthwith to surrender themselves; and also impowering the sheriff of the said county, to take such power with him, as he shall think fit and necessary, for the effectual apprehending such out-lying slave or slaves, and go in search of them: Which proclamation shall be published on a Sabbath day, at the door of every church and chapel, in the said county, by the parish clerk, or reader, of the church, immediately after divine worship: And in case any slave, against whom proclamation hath been thus issued, and once published at any church or chapel, as aforesaid, stay out, and do not immediately return home, it shall be lawful for any person or persons whatsoever, to kill and destroy such slaves by such ways and means as he, she, or they shall think fit, without accusation or impeachment of any crime for the same: And if any slave, that hath run away and lain out as aforesaid, shall be apprehended by the sheriff, or any other person, upon the application of the owner of the said slave, it shall and may be lawful for the county court, to order such punishment to the said slave, either by dismembring, or any other way, not touching his life, as they in their discretion shall think fit, for the reclaiming any such incorrigible slave, and terrifying others from the like practices.

XIX. Provided Always, and it is further enacted, That for every slave killed, in pursuance of this act, or put to death by law, the master or owner of such slave shall be paid by the public:

XX. And to the end, the true value of every slave killed, or put to death, as aforesaid, may be the better known; and by that means, the assembly the better enabled to make a suitable allowance thereupon, Be it enacted, That upon application of the master or owner of any such slave, to the court appointed for proof of public claims, the said court shall value the slave in money, and the clerk of the court shall return a certificate thereof to the assembly, with the rest of the public claims.

XXI. And for the better putting this act in due execution, and that no servants or slaves may have pretense of ignorance hereof, Be it also enacted, That the church-wardens of each parish in this her majesty's colony and dominion, at the charge of the parish, shall provide a true copy of this act, and cause entry thereof to be made in the register book of each parish respectively; and that the parish clerk, or reader of each parish, shall, on the first sermon Sundays in September and March, annually, after sermon or divine service is ended, at the door of every church and chapel in their parish, publish the same; and the sheriff of each county shall, at the next court held for the county, after the last day of February, yearly, publish this act, at the door of the court-house: And every sheriff making default herein, shall forfeit and pay six hundred pounds of tobacco; one half to her majesty, her heirs, and successors, for and towards the support of the government; and the other half to the informer. And every parish clerk, or reader, making default herein, shall, for each time so offending, forfeit and pay six hundred pounds of tobacco; one half whereof to be to the informer; and the other half to the poor of the parish, wherein such omission shall be : To be recovered, with costs, by action of debt, bill, plaint, or information, in any court of record in this her majesty's colony and dominion, wherein no essoin, protection, or wager of law, shall be allowed.

XXII. And be it further enacted, That all and every other act and acts, and every clause and article thereof, heretofore made, for so much thereof as relates to servants and slaves, or to any other matter or thing whatsoever, within the purview of this act, is and are hereby repealed, and made void, to all intents and purposes, as if the same had never been made.

XXIII. And be it further enacted, That all and every other act and acts, and every clause and article thereof, heretofore made, for so much thereof as relates to servants and slaves, or to any other matter or thing whatsoever, within the purview of this act, is and are hereby repealed, and made void, to all intents and purposes, as if the same had never been made.

Sources:

Hening, William Waller. *The Statutes at Large*. Vol. 3. Printed by and for Samuel Pleasants, 1908: 447–462.
Virtual Jamestown. http://www.virtualjamestown.org/laws1.html#51.

APPENDIX 2(A)

Of Servants and Slaves in Virginia, 1705

1– Robert Beverley, "Of the Servants and Slaves in Virginia," *The History and Present State of Virginia*, 1705 (first ed.).

2– Virginia. An Act concerning Servants and Slaves, October 1705, excerpts.

ROBERT BEVERLEY, 1705
"Of the Servants and Slaves in Virginia"

Their Servants, they distinguish by the Names of Slaves for Life, and Servants for a time.

Slaves are the Negroes, and their Posterity [children], following the condition of the Mother, according to the Maxim, *partus sequitur ventrem,* they are call'd Slaves, in Respect of the Time of their Servitude, because it is for Life.

AUTHOR'S NOTE

As per the *Free Dictionary*, in *Partus sequitur ventrem*, the offspring follow the mother. This is the law in the case of slaves and animals. But with regard to freemen, children follow the condition of the father. To group those created in the image of God and align them with animals tells me that those self-proclaimed Christians are indeed the real infidels simply pointing fingers at the wrong people.

Servants are those which serve only for a few Years, according to the time of their Indenture or the Custom of the Country. The Custom of the Country takes place upon such as have no Indentures. The Law in this Case is that if such Servants be under nineteen Years of Age, they must be brought into Court to have their Age adjudged; And from the Age they are judg'd to be of, they must serve until they reach four and twenty; But if they be adjudged upwards of nineteen, they are then only to be Servants for the Term of five Years.

The Male-Servants, and Slaves of both Sexes, are employed together in tilling and manuring the Ground, in sowing and planting Tobacco, Corn, *&c.* Some Distinction indeed is made between them in their Clothes and Food, but the Work of both is no other than what the Overseers, the Freemen, and the Planters themselves do.

Sufficient Distinction is also made between the Female-Servants, and Slaves; *for a white Woman* is rarely or never put to work in the Ground, if she be good for any thing else; and to discourage all Planters from using any Women so, their Law imposes Taxes upon Female-Servants working in the Ground, while it suffers [allows] all other white Women to be absolutely exempted; Whereas on the other hand, it is a common thing to work a *Woman Slave out of Doors*; nor does the Law make any Distinction in her Taxes, whether her Work be Abroad [outside] or at Home.

AUTHOR'S NOTE

Italics in this paragraph are mine. The phrase "for a white woman" in italics above suggests that "white" men were also on this shameful boat of "servants and slaves." If no white men or women are willing to refer to their beginnings in the United States as "slavery or servitude," the shameful reference forced on African Americans must stop immediately.

Because I have heard how strangely cruel, and severe the Service of this Country [use of slaves and servants in Virginia] is presented in some Parts of *England*, I can't forbear affirming that the Work of their

Servants and Slaves is no other than what every common Freeman does. Neither is any Servant requir'd to do more in a Day than his Overseer. And I can assure you with great Truth that generally their Slaves are not worked near so hard, nor so many Hours in a Day, as the Husbandmen and Day-laborers in *England.* An Overseer is a Man that, having served his time, has acquired the Skill and Character of an experienced Planter, and is therefore entrusted with the Direction of the Servants and Slaves.

But to complete this account of Servants, I shall give you a short Relation [account] of the Care their Laws take, that they be used as tenderly as possible.

Excerpted, images added, and spelling and some punctuation modernized by the National Humanities Center, 2006: www.nhc.rtp.nc.us/pds/pds.htm. In Robert Beverley, *The History and Present State of Virginia,* 1705, ed. Louis B. Wright (Chapel Hill: The University of North Carolina Press, published for the Institute of Early American History and Culture, Williamsburg, Virginia, 1947), Bk. IV, Ch. X, pp. 271-274. Copyright 1947 by the University of North Carolina Press; renewed 1975 by Louis B. Wright. Reproduced by permission of the publisher, www.uncpress.unc.edu. Full text of revised 2d. ed., 1722, at the Library of Congress: hdl.loc.gov/loc.gdc/lhbcb.06557. Complete image credits at www.nhc.rtp.nc.us/pds/amerbegin/imagecredits.htm.

By the Laws of their Country.[2]

1. All Servants whatsoever have their Complaints heard without Fee or Reward; but if the Master be found Faulty, the charge of the Complaint is cast upon him, otherwise the Business is done *ex Officio.*
2. Any Justice of Peace may receive the Complaint of a Servant, and order everything relating thereto, till the next County-Court, where it will be finally determin'd.
3. All Masters are under the Correction and Censure of the County-Courts, to provide for their Servants good and wholesome Diet, Clothing, and Lodging.

4. They are always to appear upon the first notice given of the Complaint of their Servants, otherwise to forfeit the Service of them, until they do appear.
5. All Servants' Complaints are to be receiv'd at any time in Court, without Process, and shall not be delay'd for want of Form; but the Merits of the Complaint must be immediately inquir'd into by the Justices; and if the Master cause any delay therein, the Court may remove such Servants, if they see Cause, until the Master will come to Trial.
6. If a Master shall at any time disobey an Order of Court made upon any Complaint of a Servant, the Court is empower'd to remove such Servant forthwith to another Master who will be kinder, giving to the former Master the Produce only (after Fees deducted) of what such Servants shall be sold for by Public Outcry.
7. If a Master should be so cruel as to use his Servant ill, that is fal[le]n sick or lame in his Service, and thereby render'd unfit for Labor, he must be remov'd by the Church-Wardens out of the way of such Cruelty and boarded in some good Planter's House, till the time of his Freedom, the Charge of which must be laid before the next County-Court, which has Power to levy the same from time to time upon the Goods and Chattels (personal property) of the Master; After which, the Charge of such Boarding is to come upon the Parish in general.
8. All hired Servants are entitled to these Privileges.
9. No Master or a Servant can make a new Bargain for Service, or other Matter with his Servant, without the privity [equal relationship in the contract] and consent of a Justice of Peace, to prevent the Master's Overreaching or scaring such Servant into an unreasonable Compliance. The property of all Money and Goods sent over thither to Servants, or carry'd in with them, is reserv'd to themselves and remains entirely at their Disposal.
10. Each Servant at his Freedom receives of his Master fifteen Bushels of Corn (which is sufficient for whole Year)[3] two new Suits of Clothes, both Linen and Woolen,[4] and then becomes

as free in all Respects, and as much entitled to the Liberties and Privileges of the Country as any other of the Inhabitants or Natives are.[5]

11. Each Servant has then also a Right to take up fifty Acres of Land, where he can find any unpatented; But that is no great Privilege, for any one may have as good a right for a piece of Eight.[6]

This is what the Laws prescribe in Favor of Servants, by which you may find that the Cruelties and Severities imputed to that Country [Virginia] are an unjust Reflection. For no People more abhor the thoughts of such Usage than the *Virginians,* nor take more Precaution to prevent it.

1 In 1662 Virginia legislated the doctrine of *partus sequitur ventrem*, which assigned a child's status as free or slave according to the status of the mother.

2 The 1705 Virginia statute regarding servants and slaves is excerpted on pages three and four of these selections.
National Humanities Center

3 In 1722 edition: "ten bushels of corn (which is sufficient for almost a Year)."

4 In 1722 edition: "and a Gun 20 *s[hillings].* value."

5 In 1722 edition: "if such Servants were not Aliens."

6 In 1722 edition, the last clause of this sentence ("But that is ... piece of Eight") is omitted.
National Humanities Center

APPENDIX 2(B)

Virginia. An Act concerning Servants and Slaves. October 1705. Excerpts.

Be it enacted, by the governor, council, and burgesses, of this present general assembly, and it is hereby enacted, by the authority of the same,

— That all servants brought into this country without indenture, if the said servants be Christians and of Christian parentage, and above nineteen years of age, shall serve but five years; and if under nineteen years of age, 'till they shall become twenty-four years of age, and no longer …

— That all servants imported and brought into this country by sea or land, who were not Christians in their native country, (except Turks and Moors in amity with her majesty, and others that can make due proof of their being free in England, or any other Christian country, before they were shipped, in order to transportation hither) shall be accounted and be slaves, and as such be here bought and sold notwithstanding a conversion to Christianity afterwards …

— That all masters and owners of servants shall find and provide for their servants wholesome and competent diet, clothing, and lodging, by the discretion of the county court; and shall not, at any time, give immoderate correction [excessive punishment]; neither shall at any time whip *a Christian white servant* naked without an order from a justice of the peace …

— That all servants (not being slaves,) whether imported or become servants of their own accord here, or bound by any court or church-wardens, shall have their complaints received by a justice of the peace, who, if he find cause, shall bind the master over to answer the complaint at court …

— *That no negros, mulattos, or Indians, although Christians, or Jews, Moors, Mahometans [Muslims], or other infidels shall at any time purchase any Christian servant, nor any other, except of their own complexion or such as are declared slaves by this act …*

AUTHOR'S NOTE

Italics in the paragraphs above are mine. As pointed out earlier, who are these so-called Negros and others hereby forbidden from having a "Christian servant"? Do not forget that "Christian white servant" is defined in the previous chapter. Please remember that this act clearly states that some Negros are forbidden from having Christian servants. If slaves are slaves forever, what does that tells you? This should tell you that not all black people came here as slaves. Just as some white people came to this country as free men and women, so did some blacks. We cannot deny the fact that some were brought here as slaves. If we cannot identify those so-called whites or are willing to group all whites as slaves or servants, the false history of slavery assigned to *all* black people should henceforth come to an end.

The time has come to remember and recognize those Africans who came here as explorers and sojourners, thereby respecting and acknowledging their contributions. The selfish accolades and respect assigned to Europeans at the expense of Africans has to come to an end. This is our land too, and we all deserve to see our names in print and our statues go up as free men and women.

— That there shall be paid and allowed to every imported servant, not having yearly wages, at the time of service ended, by the master or owner of such servant, viz: To every male servant, ten bushels of Indian corn, thirty shillings in money, or the value thereof in goods, and one well fixed musket or fuzee, of the value of twenty shillings, at least: and to every woman servant, fifteen bushels of Indian corn and forty shillings in money, or the value thereof in goods …

— That in all cases of penal laws, whereby persons free are punishable by fine, *servants shall be punished by whipping*, after the rate of twenty lashes for every five hundred pounds of tobacco, or fifty shillings current money, unless the servant so culpable can and will procure some person or persons to pay the fine; in which case, the said servant shall be adjudged to serve such benefactor after the time by indenture, custom, or order of court, to *his or her then present master or owner,* shall be expired …

AUTHOR'S NOTE

Italics here are also mine. If you think *servant* is a better label, look carefully at the italicized phrases, and you will discover that they have masters and owners. This constitutes slavery under the auspices of servitude.

Take a careful look at the next paragraph, and you will also see that not all English or other European men and women came here as free men and women. It also explicitly shows that not all Negros or mulattos are slaves.

Slavery is not unique and exclusive to just one ethnic group. It is without doubt a human dilemma. Any reference to it should be stricken and the memory of it erased, thereby allowing all God's children to enjoy their God-given pride in who they are and their divinely ordained free volition. No one is superior, and no one is inferior.

— That whatsoever *English or other white man or woman, being free*, shall intermarry with a *negro or mulatto man or woman, bond or free*, shall by judgment of the county court be committed to prison and there remain during the space of six months, without bail or mainprize; and shall forfeit and pay ten pounds current money of Virginia, to the use of the parish …

— And *if any slave resist his master or owner* or other person, by his or her order, correcting such slave, and shall happen to be killed in such correction, it shall not be accounted felony; but the master, owner, and every such other person so giving correction shall be free and acquit of all punishment and accusation for the same, as if such accident had never happened; And also, if any negro, mulatto, or Indian, bond or free, shall at any time lift his or her hand in opposition against any Christian, not being negro, mulatto, or Indian, he or she so offending shall, for every such offence proved by the oath of the party, receive on his or her bare back thirty lashes, well laid on; cognizable by a justice of the peace for that county wherein such offense shall be committed …

— That no slave go armed with gun, sword, club, staff, or other weapon, nor go from off the plantation and seat of land where such slave shall be appointed to live, without a certificate of leave in writing for so doing from his or her master, mistress, or overseer: And if any slave shall be found offending herein, it shall be lawful for any person or persons to apprehend and deliver such slave to the next constable or head-borough, who is hereby enjoined and required, without further order or warrant, to give such slave twenty lashes on his or her bare back, well laid on, and so send him or her home …

— That baptism of slaves does not exempt them from bondage; and that all children shall be bond or free, according to the condition of their mothers, and the particular directions of this act.

University of Virginia Library

AUTHOR'S NOTE

The census information you are about to read, which was provided by the United States Census Bureau with the help of the Library of Congress, clearly shows the fact that both free Africans as well as those who were brought here as slaves were included in the census of 1790 and beyond. It also shows Africans who were *slave-holding families* even in 1790. The earliest slave-holding families (slave owners of white slaves) were discouraged and stopped as a result of the state of Virginia law of 1705. Is there any reason why those free and slave-holding families' efforts and contributions are not being celebrated? Is there any reason why they were forgotten, neglected by historians, and treated as unimportant and inconsequential? Why are these not available in any museums, even the Smithsonian and African American Museum of History? If you cannot trust the Smithsonian to give us a true story of the past, where else can you go? They too intentionally allowed misnomers to exist.

What you see in the outcome of the census shown below contradicts that false information published and released in Virginia relating to the recorded 12.5 million Africans transported to the United States as slaves. There are some places designated as a "point of no return" on the continent of Africa. Are there any similar places in Europe or any other continent?

Take a careful look at what was recorded for Virginia and West Virginia in 1790. What happened to that exaggerated 12.5 million Africans who supposedly were brought to the United States a little over one hundred years prior? Were they erroneously or intentionally omitted in the census? I challenge historians to come up with a credible explanation.

FACT

1. The true history of African Americans has nothing to do with slavery but much to do with the following:
   a. exploration
   b. discovery
   c. land occupation
2. Those European latecomers who intentionally twisted the truth in the interest of impressing those who sent them did so without any sense of guilt. As a result, they came up with selfish, self-glorifying, and misleading reports, which were sent to the king and queen of England. They intentionally assigned the misleading title of "first" in everything to themselves and willfully disregarded Africans who came before them. As a result, truth was intentionally swept off and thought forgotten.
3. The mysterious label of "house slave" erroneously made popular in the African American communities was developed by those who wanted to disregard and demean the pride of those neglected and forgotten in the history of African American slave owners.
4. The same census information shown below refers to "decennial census." You may be wondering what decennial census is all about. It started in 1790, as required by the US Constitution, Article 1, Section 2. It was mainly for the purpose of apportioning the US House of Representatives. As revealed by the US Census Bureau, "data collected by the decennial census are used to determine the number of seats each state has in the U.S. House of Representatives." Africans being included in this census at that time was not a mistake. It was done because *they were free and productive members* of their country, the United States of America.

Gerrymandering (a deceiving law made to further divide by redistricting citizens) came afterward with the intent to restructure and thereby redistribute what the decennial census already allowed. If I may repeat, "privileged group never give up their privileges without some resistant." In the end, no matter what, the extraordinary resilience and inner resolve of all agents of light will no doubt help the truth to prevail.

TRUTH BURIED BY HISTORIANS

According to the Census Bureau, information regarding free colored persons and slaves were revealed at each decennial census from 1790 – 1860. This was a few years before Emancipation Proclamation written and released by President Lincoln. Decennial census as a "classification was essential to the observations of a specific article of the Constitution, which directed that representation in the House should be apportioned to the several States according to their population, including in the apportionment population all free persons except Indians …"

Other facts revealed indicates:

- "At the census of 1790 slaves were reported from all the states and territories enumerated with the exception of Vermont and Massachusetts." Maine was at that time a district of Massachusetts. Some of the outcome revealed can be found on the table (shown on the next page as Figure 1) obtained from the Census Bureau.
    - o *This information did not agree with the bogus claim of historians that 12.5 million Africans brought to the United States as slaves after the initial number of 19 in 1619*
- More than one-fifth of "the Negro" population were free.
    - o *How come this information cannot be found in history book?*
- "The increase of the free colored population" revealed in the same Census was due in part to "natural increase by excess of births over deaths among the free colored" people.

- As per the census of 1860, **7,011** free colored persons "were foreign born" and about 3,700 or more were reported to have chosen the state of New York as their resident of choice.
  - o *This is another indication and undeniable fact that not all Africans came here as slaves. However, is any historian aware of the fact that these foreign born freely came even before the Statue of Liberty built by Gustave Eiffel was given as a gift to the United States by France? "How long will prejudice blind the visions of men?"*
- The census of 1790, "which are in existence" and one of it shown below in Figure 2 reported a "total of 5,161 free colored families of which 195 are designated as slave-holding families." In the interest of clarity, these were African slave owners

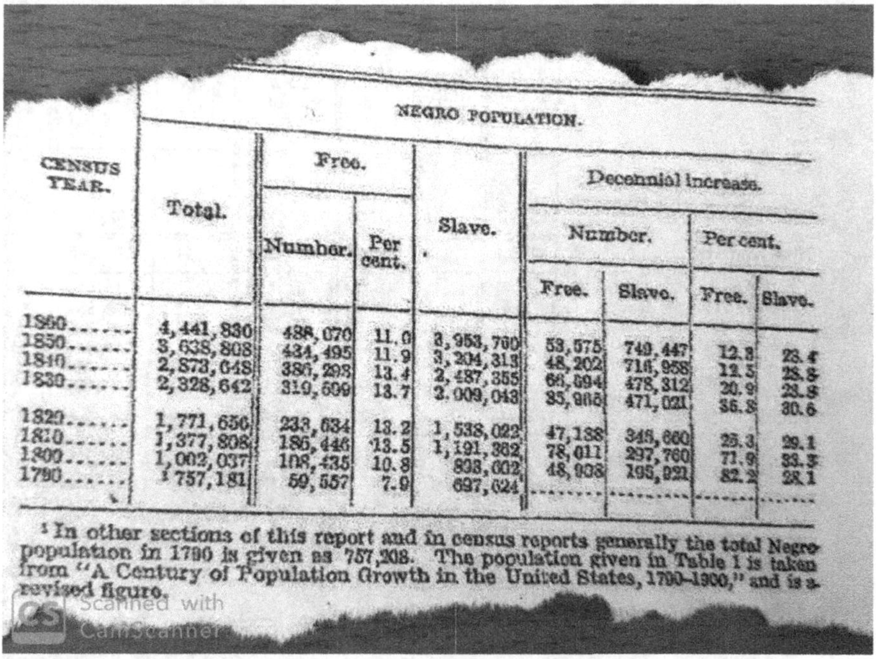

Census year.	Negro population. Total.	Free. Number.	Free. Per cent.	Slave.	Decennial increase. Number. Free.	Decennial increase. Number. Slave.	Decennial increase. Per cent. Free.	Decennial increase. Per cent. Slave.
1860......	4,441,830	488,070	11.0	3,953,760	53,575	749,447	12.3	23.4
1850......	3,638,808	434,495	11.9	3,204,313	48,202	716,958	12.5	28.8
1840......	2,873,648	386,293	13.4	2,487,355	66,694	478,312	20.9	23.8
1830......	2,328,642	319,599	13.7	2,009,043	85,965	471,021	36.8	30.6
1820......	1,771,656	233,634	13.2	1,538,022	47,138	346,660	25.3	29.1
1810......	1,377,808	186,446	13.5	1,191,362	78,011	297,760	71.9	33.3
1800......	1,002,037	108,435	10.8	893,602	48,938	195,921	82.2	28.1
1790......	[1] 757,181	59,557	7.9	697,624	....	....	....	....

[1] In other sections of this report and in census reports generally the total Negro population in 1790 is given as 757,208. The population given in Table 1 is taken from "A Century of Population Growth in the United States, 1790-1900," and is a revised figure.

Figure 1 Actual population of Africans in the USA 1790 - 1860

DIVISION AND STATE.	PRIVATE FAMILIES: 1790.[1] Free colored. Total number.	Free colored. Slaveholding.	Free colored. Nonslaveholding.	White. Total number.	White. Slaveholding.	White. Nonslaveholding.
Area covered by 1790 schedules in existence	5,161	195	4,966	405,475	47,664	357,811
New England	1,634	6	1,628	172,383	2,141	170,242
Maine	37	....	37	16,972	....	16,972
New Hampshire	83	....	83	23,982	123	23,859
Vermont	23	....	23	14,969	....	14,969
Massachusetts	630	....	630	65,149	....	65,149
Rhode Island	442	....	442	10,854	461	10,393
Connecticut	419	6	413	40,457	1,557	38,900
Middle states	1,245	16	1,229	127,507	9,638	117,869
New York	693	9	684	54,185	7,787	46,398
Pennsylvania	552	7	545	73,322	1,851	71,471
Southern states	2,282	173	2,109	105,585	35,885	69,700
Maryland [2]	1,282	84	1,198	32,012	12,142	19,870
North Carolina [3]	680	28	652	48,021	14,945	33,076
South Carolina	320	61	259	25,552	8,798	16,754

[1] Data not available for New Jersey, Delaware, Virginia, Georgia, Kentucky, or Southwest Territory.
[2] Data not available for Allegany, Calvert, or Somerset Counties.
[3] Data not available for Caswell, Granville, or Orange Counties, except the total number of families.

Figure 2 Free Africans and Africans who were slave owners

FREE COLORED AND SLAVE POPULATION.

—NEGRO POPULATION, SLAVE AND FREE, AT EACH CENSUS BY DIVISIONS AND STATES: 1790-1860.

DIVISION AND STATE.	NEGRO POPULATION. 1860		1850		1840		1830		1820		1810		1800		1790	
	Slave.	Free.	Slave.	Free.	Slave.	Free.	Slave.	Free.	Slave.	Free.	Slave.	Free.	Slave.	Free.	Slave.	Free.
UNITED STATES	3,953,760	488,070	3,204,313	434,495	2,487,355	386,293	2,009,043	319,599	1,538,022	233,634	1,191,362	186,446	893,602	108,435	697,624	59,557
GEOGRAPHIC DIVISIONS:																
New England	...	24,711	...	23,021	23	22,634	48	21,331	145	20,782	418	19,488	1,339	17,313	3,763	13,059
Middle Atlantic	18	131,272	236	126,505	742	118,925	2,732	101,103	17,856	71,941	26,663	55,668	35,031	29,383	36,323	13,975
East North Central	...	63,699	...	45,195	348	28,997	788	15,095	1,107	6,584	429	3,025	135	500	...	...
West North Central	114,948	5,592	87,422	2,990	58,256	1,746	25,091	569	10,222	347	3,011	607	...	...	...	...
South Atlantic	1,840,445	217,753	1,663,397	197,474	1,425,539	171,778	1,376,196	153,087	1,156,479	116,920	983,997	96,803	799,681	60,909	641,691	32,048
East South Central	1,372,913	21,447	1,103,162	19,628	814,060	16,246	490,024	11,563	281,532	6,525	142,184	3,270	57,416	1,230	15,847	475
West South Central	625,407	19,146	350,070	18,467	188,387	25,967	114,164	16,851	70,681	10,535	34,660	7,585	...	...	...	...
Mountain	29	206	26	46	...	...	...	...	...	...	...	...	...	...	...	...
Pacific	...	4,244	...	1,169	...	...	...	...	...	...	...	...	...	...	...	...
NEW ENGLAND:																
Maine	...	1,327	...	1,356	...	1,355	2	1,190	...	929	...	969	...	818	...	536
New Hampshire	...	494	...	520	1	537	3	604	...	786	...	970	8	852	157	630
Vermont	...	709	...	718	...	730	...	881	...	903	...	750	...	557	...	269
Massachusetts	...	9,602	...	9,064	...	8,669	1	7,048	...	6,740	...	6,737	...	6,452	...	5,369
Rhode Island	...	3,952	...	3,670	5	3,238	17	3,561	48	3,554	108	3,609	380	3,304	958	3,484
Connecticut	...	8,627	...	7,693	17	8,105	25	8,047	97	7,870	310	6,453	951	5,330	2,648	2,771
MIDDLE ATLANTIC:																
New York	...	49,005	...	49,069	4	50,027	75	44,870	10,088	29,279	15,017	25,333	20,903	10,417	21,193	4,682
New Jersey	18	25,318	236	23,810	674	21,044	2,254	18,303	7,557	12,460	10,851	7,843	12,422	4,402	11,423	2,762
Pennsylvania	...	56,949	...	53,626	64	47,854	403	37,930	211	30,202	795	22,492	1,706	14,564	3,707	6,531
EAST NORTH CENTRAL:																
Ohio	...	36,673	...	25,279	3	17,342	6	9,568	...	4,723	...	1,899	...	337	...	...
Indiana	...	11,428	...	11,262	3	7,165	3	3,629	190	1,230	237	393	135	163	...	...
Illinois	...	7,628	...	5,436	331	3,598	747	1,637	917	457	168	613	...	...	...	...
Michigan	...	6,799	...	2,583	...	707	32	261	...	174	24	120	...	...	...	...
Wisconsin	...	1,171	...	635	11	185	...	...	...	...	...	...	...	...	...	...
WEST NORTH CENTRAL:																
Minnesota	...	259	...	39	...	...	...	...	...	...	...	...	...	...	...	...
Iowa	...	1,069	...	333	16	172	...	...	...	...	...	...	...	...	...	...
Missouri	114,931	3,572	87,422	2,618	58,240	1,574	25,091	569	10,222	347	3,011	607	...	...	...	...
North Dakota	...	...	...	...	...	...	...	...	...	...	...	...	...	...	...	...
South Dakota	...	...	...	...	...	...	...	...	...	...	...	...	...	...	...	...
Nebraska	15	67	...	...	...	...	...	...	...	...	...	...	...	...	...	...
Kansas	2	625	...	...	...	...	...	...	...	...	...	...	...	...	...	...
SOUTH ATLANTIC:																
Delaware	1,798	19,829	2,290	18,073	2,605	16,919	3,292	15,855	4,509	12,958	4,177	13,136	6,153	8,268	8,887	3,899
Maryland	87,189	83,942	90,368	74,723	89,737	62,078	102,994	52,938	107,397	39,730	111,502	33,927	105,635	19,587	103,036	8,043
District of Columbia	3,185	11,131	3,687	10,059	4,694	8,361	6,119	6,152	6,377	4,048	5,395	2,549	3,244	783	...	...
Virginia	490,865	58,042	472,528	54,333	448,987	49,842	469,757	47,348	425,148	36,883	392,516	30,570	345,796	20,124	292,627	12,866
West Virginia	...	...	...	...	...	...	...	...	...	...	...	...	...	...	...	...
North Carolina	331,059	30,463	288,548	27,463	245,817	22,732	245,601	19,543	204,917	14,712	168,824	10,266	133,296	7,043	100,783	5,041
South Carolina	402,406	9,914	384,984	8,960	327,038	8,276	315,401	7,921	258,475	6,826	196,365	4,554	146,151	3,185	107,094	1,801
Georgia	462,198	3,500	381,682	2,931	280,944	2,753	217,531	2,486	149,656	1,763	105,218	1,801	59,406	1,019	29,264	398
Florida	61,745	932	39,310	932	25,717	817	15,501	844	...	...	...	...	...	...	...	...
EAST SOUTH CENTRAL:																
Kentucky	225,483	10,684	210,981	10,011	182,258	7,317	165,213	4,917	126,732	2,759	80,561	1,713	40,343	739	12,430	114
Tennessee	275,719	7,300	239,459	6,422	183,059	5,524	141,603	4,555	80,107	2,737	44,535	1,317	13,584	309	3,417	361
Alabama	435,080	2,690	342,844	2,265	253,532	2,039	117,549	1,572	41,879	571	...	...	...	...	...	...
Mississippi	436,631	773	309,878	930	195,211	1,366	65,659	519	32,814	458	17,088	240	3,489	182	...	...
WEST SOUTH CENTRAL:																
Arkansas	111,115	144	47,100	608	19,935	465	4,576	141	1,617	59	...	...	...	...	...	...
Louisiana	331,726	18,647	244,809	17,462	168,452	25,502	109,588	16,710	69,064	10,476	34,660	7,585	...	...	...	...
Oklahoma	...	...	...	...	...	...	...	...	...	...	...	...	...	...	...	...
Texas	182,566	355	58,161	397	...	...	...	...	...	...	...	...	...	...	...	...
MOUNTAIN:																
Montana	...	...	...	...	...	...	...	...	...	...	...	...	...	...	...	...
Idaho	...	...	...	...	...	...	...	...	...	...	...	...	...	...	...	...
Wyoming	...	...	...	...	...	...	...	...	...	...	...	...	...	...	...	...
Colorado	...	46	...	...	...	...	...	...	...	...	...	...	...	...	...	...
New Mexico	...	85	...	22	...	...	...	...	...	...	...	...	...	...	...	...
Arizona	...	...	...	...	...	...	...	...	...	...	...	...	...	...	...	...
Utah	29	30	26	24	...	...	...	...	...	...	...	...	...	...	...	...
Nevada	...	45	...	...	...	...	...	...	...	...	...	...	...	...	...	...
PACIFIC:																
Washington	...	30	...	...	...	...	...	...	...	...	...	...	...	...	...	...
Oregon	...	128	...	207	...	...	...	...	...	...	...	...	...	...	...	...
California	...	4,086	...	962	...	...	...	...	...	...	...	...	...	...	...	...

Figure 3 Comprehensive population 1790 – 1860

Printed in the United States
By Bookmasters